D1070833

THE
REINVENTION
FORMULA

FOREWORD BY **JON GORDON**

CRAIG SIEGEL

THE
REINVENTION
FORMULA

HOW TO **UNLOCK A BULLETPROOF MINDSET** TO **UPGRADE YOUR LIFE**

WILEY

For general information on our other products and services or for technical support, please contact our Customer Care Department within the United States at (800) 762-2974, outside the United States at (317) 572-3993 or fax (317) 572-4002.

Wiley also publishes its books in a variety of electronic formats. Some content that appears in print may not be available in electronic formats. For more information about Wiley products, visit our web site at www.wiley.com.

Library of Congress Cataloging-in-Publication Data:

Names: Siegel, Craig, author.
Title: The reinvention formula : how to unlock a bulletproof mindset to
   upgrade your life / Craig Siegel.
Description: Hoboken, New Jersey : Wiley, [2023] | Includes index.
Identifiers: LCCN 2023016783 (print) | LCCN 2023016784 (ebook) | ISBN
   9781394182107 (cloth) | ISBN 9781394182466 (adobe pdf) | ISBN
   9781394182114 (epub)
Subjects: LCSH: Identity (Psychology) | Self-realization.
Classification: LCC BF697 .S543 2023 (print) | LCC BF697 (ebook) | DDC
   155.2--dc23/eng/20230607
LC record available at https://lccn.loc.gov/2023016783
LC ebook record available at https://lccn.loc.gov/2023016784

Cover Design and Image: Wiley
Author Photo: Photographed by Lisa Richov

SKY10049941_063023

I humbly dedicate this book to my family—my parents and my brother Marc, as well as my fiancée, Olesya—for the creation of this book. My parents' unwavering love and support for me throughout my life has contributed a great deal to my success, and their beautiful core values will always be ingrained in my DNA. My best friend and brother Marc, is the perfect sibling who has always been my biggest fan, cheerleader, and confidant. Olesya, my heart, is my person, my soulmate, and my copilot in life. I hope everyone has a rock of support like the one I've been blessed with. My inner circle is the foundation of my identity and a big part of the rise of CLS and more specifically my reinvention. I love each of you with every ounce of me and hope you find great joy and pride in what we've created here. We're just getting warmed up.

For the person who feels stuck right now, feels unhappy and unfulfilled, as if you know you are here for a much bigger purpose but you can't seem to find your way; or you think you're too old or it's too late; or happiness, impact, and abundance just isn't in the cards for you; then I want you to know this: You are absolutely valued, appreciated, and here by no coincidence, your best is yet to come, and reinvention is ready when you are.

Contents

Foreword

If you feel stuck or that it's too late to change or that your dream life will never happen, I'm glad you are reading this book!

Craig Siegel is the embodiment of reinvention and transformation. After a 13-year career on Wall Street he transformed pain into purpose, the mundane into meaning, and drifting into drive by reinventing himself with a new mission and purpose to impact the lives of others.

As someone who went from being a miserable restaurant owner and unfulfilled entrepreneur in the emerging world of wireless software 23 years ago to becoming a 14x best-selling author and speaker, I relate to Craig's valuable experience, powerful messages, and life-changing lessons. I had to reinvent myself as Craig did, and I'm thankful he has created a formula that anyone who is unhappy with their life and career can apply for a new beginning.

It's never too late to create the life that you want and become all that you are meant to be. You just have to be willing to take action and have the courage to change. And this is why this book is so important. It gives you the inspiration, encouragement, belief, and formula to make the changes you are fearful of making. Overcoming fear is the greatest battle you will face on your path to your destiny and victory. We all need encouragers and guides along the way, and with this book you have a master guide in Craig Siegel.

A guide goes before you. They have navigated the challenging path you now face. They went through it so they can now help you through it. Craig Siegel's message and lessons resonate so deeply because he has walked the walk and now his talk hits deep and spreads far and wide.

I remember the first time I saw one of Craig's messages and videos on social media. I was, like, *Who is this guy?* He caught my attention. I knew there was something special about him. He wasn't a pretender. He was the real deal with the heart to serve and impact others. Since then, I have seen his career and impact skyrocket and I'm not surprised.

While Craig's new career was taking off he was also bringing everyone along with him. He was miserable when focused on himself and knew happiness is doing life with others and helping them get better. He knows, as I wrote in *The Carpenter,* "You aren't a true success unless you help others be successful."

And what does it mean to be a successful?

As David Jeremiah says, "Success is the fulfillment of God's plan for your life."

If you feel like there's more for you it's because there is an inner voice telling you that you were meant for and created for more. God has always been in the reinvention and transformation business and thankfully so is Craig Siegel.

I'm thrilled you are reading this book that Craig wrote to help you create the successful life you were born to live. Don't wait for it to happen. Start creating it today!

Jon Gordon
14x Best-Selling Author of *The Energy Bus, The Seed,*
and *The Power of Positive Leadership*

Preface

You will never influence the world by trying to be like it.

             – *Sean McCabe*

Spoiler Alert

It's true, we're gonna dive deep on all the tools, strategies, mindset shifts, stories, principles, and lessons required to totally reinvent yourself in this world. However, just like the self-help-event junkies I've come to know, please understand that knowledge is not power, it's potential power pending on what you do with it. You must be available to both receive the nuggets, and go all in on the concepts and tactics. It's not enough to just consume the content here. You must digest and apply it. Let's make a promise right now before we go any further. We're not gonna just be interested in the teachings inside this book, we're gonna be committed. In fact, we're going to be all in to level up, push way past our current comfort zones, to really take uncomfortable and messy action. Deal? Okay, great!

That said, I'll never *tell you* to follow me. I prefer that you come *with* me, to a whole new life of abundance, blessings, being at the right place at the right time, having the wrong people exit your life in a timely fashion, form the right relationships, the creative divine downloads and a new-found unwavering self-belief and courage to identify your God-given gifts, and fulfill your assignment by making a massive impact on this world. Without further ado, let's have some fun, stretch our perceived limitations, and get both weird and nuts over the course of The Reinvention Formula. Showtime, baby.

Who Is Craig Siegel and What Triggered His Reinvention?

Your light is gonna irritate a lot of unhealed people.

– Author unknown

I grew up with no clarity. I wasn't one of those kids who identified from an early age who I was or who I wanted to become or even a career path. Both my parents, who I absolutely adore, kept my brother and me in a bit of a bubble. I was naive and didn't understand how life works. I was a popular kid, was always joking around and loved to laugh, and was definitely not the best student. I had street smarts, as you will soon discover, where I picked up many entrepreneurial endeavors such as selling weed, taking sports bets, shoveling snow in the winter, and trading sports cards. I always had ambition, but it wasn't congruent with real-life impact and contributions. I played sports often, although I wouldn't consider myself very athletic, until later in life when I developed a healthy obsession with the sport of running. I was short and built up insecurities because of my height, acne, and more. I was always charismatic and had a lot of friends, just not necessarily the best influences, but I own that and take accountability for choosing them. I started to develop an edge when I realized I had a strong maniacal drive for anything I was passionate about. The problem was those passions were hard to find.

I was a fun kid, with a lack of direction and inspiration. I went to college at the University of Hartford in Connecticut, where I created a new set of friends and had fun. If I'm being honest, I didn't learn a whole lot in college from an academic standpoint and I'll own that for not taking it too seriously, but the truth is I wasn't interested in any of my subjects and classes. I'm on a mission to facilitate more personal development and entrepreneurship to be taught in school, especially at an earlier age. Education means more than just schooling. I never joined a fraternity because I was never into being hazed or treated less than my own self-worth. I did, however, have the best of both worlds because I was good friends with all the different frats yet had none of the responsibilities or distractions. That was a fun time, but the most valuable education I got from school was being on my own, experiencing life away from home, and developing responsibilities and independence. I'm not super proud of some of the choices I made these first 20 years as I was working on myself and my identity, but I also wouldn't have changed a thing because these times shaped me, built me, and helped me cultivate an edge—I knew I was here for more, and I'd never give up working toward figuring it out. I think it's important to acknowledge my brother Marc here as well. I grew up in a very close family, with an older brother who played both the role of my true best friend and my role model. My brother and I are the closest set of siblings in the world—a bold statement, I know.

I graduated college and the next season of life began, where I would finally cultivate an identity, work ethic, and experience a ton of ups and downs. But first, I want to emphasize that I actually cared about how people perceived me or what they thought of me. This made a massive impact on my identity, leaving me with a sense that I lacked worthiness, but it also created that edge I mentioned earlier. It was as though I had a small flame burning inside me that began to grow little by little and ignite in both depth and volume.

After college I didn't have a concrete game plan. I came back to my parents' house and searched for an identity and path. I spent most of my days watching the stock market while laying on an obscenely oversized recliner in my small bedroom. This thing was half the size of my little room. I'll never forget the look on my mom's face when I had it delivered one day without giving her any sort of heads up. I'm laughing just thinking of this moment right now. My mom and I often didn't see eye to eye during this season of my life. I don't blame her one bit. I was immature and underachieving. It was pretty pathetic. Who was I? No idea just yet. I struggled with identity. Buckle up, Wall Street, here I come.

1

Wall Street

Rock bottom will teach you lessons that mountaintops never will.
– Author unknown

I BECAME SICK and tired of being sick and tired and got a job as a stockbroker on Wall Street through a good friend at a firm. Much more importantly here, while looking for inspiration and an upgraded identity, I stumbled upon personal development. Pivotal Life Moment right here. This moment changed the perception of what I grew up believing was in reach or possible for me. While searching motivational videos on YouTube, I remember discovering Eric Thomas,[1] the hip-hop preacher, and watching exciting remixed videos consisting of inspirational speeches from movies such as *Rocky* (the best movie series ever) and the *Dark Knight* trilogy. I am a massive movie nerd to this day, by the way, and those Batman movies made a massive impact on me. I was fascinated with positive affirmations and began to understand that besides becoming physically fit, even more importantly we can become mentally fit. This was a game changer in my life.

It was at this moment I realized I could rewrite my story. I began to build my business, but more importantly I began to cultivate an identity and evolve. I learned the power of a strong work ethic, being super positive and optimistic and being committed and becoming open to limitless possibilities that await a healthy and positive mindset. Wall Street was a season of my life when, although I was working on myself, I was still unenlightened enough that I measured success by how much money I made. Looking back now I know that was naive of me but I was young, had no mentorship, and was figuring things out on my own. I give myself grace because I didn't know what I didn't know. In fact, we all need to give ourselves grace for some of our identities and skin we have shed. They play a role in our life stories. Wall Street stopped being fun, and the unpredictability and stress began to far exceed any of the positives. But something still remained. My personal development journey was gaining momentum, and I was obsessed with growth.

Eventually I discovered that Wall Street wasn't in alignment with who I was becoming, and I left to begin a new business as an owner, where we provided working capital to businesses across the country.

I brought all my upgraded personality traits and character developments with me.

With my new business underway I found it challenging to reenergize my fire within and wake up excited the way I had years prior. I realized that change can be good but it also must be in alignment with who you are becoming, and my new venture, although lucrative, was not interesting, exciting, or fulfilling to me the way I dreamed a career should be. And you better believe a career should be something you love, because you're gonna spend a lot of time in it over the course of your life.

This led to a dark season because, although I had developed motivation and ways to "sharpen the axe" (meaning to work on myself), read books, and accumulate knowledge, I lacked any real purpose and inspiration at my new endeavor. I honestly was never excited about it, but I needed a fresh start and some kind of change of scenery. Being a boss was fun, and I enjoyed helping my employees grow both personally and professionally. During these times, my morning motivational meetings with the troops were some of my favorite parts of this season. As it turns out, the writing was on the wall, but we'll come back to that. As much as I tried to sell myself on this new industry, the fact of the matter was, it wasn't in alignment with me nor with the person I was growing into. The person I was during this season was someone who was attracting poor choices. You don't manifest what you want, you manifest what you are. Don't ever forget that—in fact, highlight it, or write it down, or both!

Around this time in 2018, I was going through quite a bit. It felt like a dark cloud hovered over me for a couple years. My dad, my best friend and hero, had been healthy his entire life. Now as an older gentleman, he had a stroke, which led to the discovery of lung cancer. His doctor did not have a positive bedside manner and the prognosis was not great. I was also in a toxic relationship that I knew wasn't right, but I felt stuck. My advice there is that being single is absolutely okay and a beautiful season. Don't ever settle if you know deep down it's not the right fit. I also started drinking more than I'd like to admit to numb my misery and unhappiness. I made some poor investments, found myself in about $80,000 in credit card debt and was the poster boy for rock bottom. Sadly, Mondays were my least favorite day of the week (they're now my favorite) and quite frankly I didn't love myself. I was in pain. Trust me, emotional pain is harder than physical pain. I felt stuck in many areas and struggled to climb out or find any real excitement or new direction. I take full accountability and ownership for this season but I'm grateful for the darkness that helped me want to see the light. I was at a low point also known as rock bottom. Here's the good news. From down there, you can only go in one direction—up.

Ask Yourself: What challenging life moments helped shape you into the person you are today?

Note

1. https://podcasts.apple.com/us/podcast/you-owe-you-with-eric-thomas/
   id1533716044?i=1000580730105

2

Marathon Season

No one is ever defeated until defeat has been accepted as a reality.

— Bruce Lee

To THIS DAY I don't know if I found running or running found me. It was divine and beautiful. I was desperate for an outlet. I started to gain the perspective that if I could just get some momentum I could not only climb out of this darkness, but I could become available for the beautiful abundance the world is full of. One day after consistently lifting weights for 15 years, I was feeling frisky and I went for a run. I was humbled with the challenge of completing 2 miles, breathing heavily, and turning a respectable jog into a power walk to finish. I went home that night and immediately cultivated a deep curiosity for the sport. Was I just not in great physical athletic shape? Or was I a long way from being anything remotely close to being mentally fit? As it turns out it was the latter.

The next day I relentlessly set out to conquer a 5k (3.1 miles) run without stopping. I did a bit better and became obsessed with this newfound sport. From there I started to Google everything about running. I even picked up *Spartan Up*, a book by my now friend Joe De Sena,[1] the founder of The Spartan Empire. This season of life provided a newfound passion and purpose for running and what it takes to be successful at the sport. I'm romantic about running. I love that it's just you, God, your thoughts, and the road. The sport requires no opponent, it's just you versus you, and battling the sometimes-negative voice in your head. It blossomed into a moving meditation for me during which I would do my best thinking and deepest inner work. I signed up for an official 5k on Long Island, completed that, and moved on to a 10k (6.2 miles). My obsessive personality is totally used for good here, because running provided so many positive life lessons and more productive behaviors. I began to learn about nutrition, hopped on a meal plan, started incorporating rest and recovery, and only had a cocktail once in a while. For the readers here, I believe physical goals are so important not because of the actual goal itself, but who we become in the pursuit: healthier, better decision-making and disciplined human beings.

After the scheduled 10k was completed, by now I think you know what was on my radar next. If you're gonna think, you might as well think BIG. Another life lesson that would become a part of my DNA was thinking huge and focusing on what could go right as opposed to what could go wrong—conditioning I really had to first unlearn and then relearn to harness as a superpower: thinking BIG.

I made a decision to sign up for the TCS NYC Marathon: 26.2 miles and 5 boroughs of road, bridges, and New York's loudest and most loyal. I wanted to really test myself at this season of life. I felt that, if I could pull this off with minimal running experience, I could use it as a point of reference for other spectacular life events and opportunities. I would also have the chance to inspire my dad who was battling the late stage diagnosis of cancer, which was scary, tough on the body, and devastating to the mindset. So, although an audacious goal, I was ready to swing for the fences with a ton of upside and growth waiting for me on the other side.

My next move was to assume massive accountability by declaring and posting about this moonshot and raising money for a charity in order to enter the race. This was a monster life lesson and applicable for anyone in any arena of life. When you tell people about your audacious goal, it suddenly becomes alive. It has energy. It has a pulse and a vibration. There's a lot at stake when we create outside expectations in addition to our inner expectations. This is one of the most brave and courageous things we can do as humans: tell the world what we intend to do and then set out to accomplish it. The extra surge of accountability here is heavy and real. You may be able to let yourself down behind closed doors, but now that the world knows about it, it becomes a non-negotiable. This is powerful and a cheat code to dig even deeper.

That season was so beautiful. I started to cultivate a new identity and self-belief that really gained momentum like a small snowball rolling down a snowy mountain and picking up more mass and speed. Truth be told I didn't have a ton of strategy for this race, but where I lacked strategy I doubled down on heart and grit, two extremely powerful characteristics for a meaningful and successful life.

Showtime—here we go—the day arrived and I was ready to be a gladiator in the arena of running and also life. I remember walking up to the start line corral as they blasted one of my favorite songs by Florence and the Machine called "Shake It Out" where I started to cry and was blitzed with an avalanche of emotions. I remember saying to myself, "How amazing God is." A lot can change in a short amount of time. Here we go baby, Frank Sinatra's "New York, New York" now blasting while 50,000 strong set out for different reasons all with the common goal to showcase the human spirit on fire and bravely run. The marathon is so beautiful. If you don't plan on running one, I highly suggest being a spectator at one. It's emotional, full of blood, sweat, tears and spirit as everyone has a different why for entering. It's amazing what we can accomplish. The marathon will humble you and can be your best friend or your worst enemy, but you'll be better for the experience, period, end of story.

I finished that marathon with family and friends cheering me on, my mom crying, of course—she always cries. I remember crossing the finish line and checking the time and feeling the most unique hybrid of emotions consisting of tremendous pride and yet showered with disappointment. I ran a 4:12 and failed to break the symbolic milestone of running under four hours. With one marathon under my belt, a new found sense of accomplishment and confidence, I was getting closer to reinventing myself and transforming into an impactful, world contributing juggernaut of a human. I had grown so much during this season and fell in love with the process that finishing a marathon—which was once the goal—was now not nearly enough. I had to break four hours and evolve even more, shedding old patterns, identities, and skin. Just doing something was no longer good enough, so doing something at an elite level with no limitations or lack of belief was the new standard. As of the writing of this book, I've conquered a total of six marathons with a personal record (PR) last month (October 2022) in Chicago of 3:31:25. We'll circle back to this season with more to come from the running journey and beautiful life lessons included.

Ask Yourself: What hobbies or passions in your life are you curious about taking to the next level?

Note

1. https://podcasts.apple.com/us/podcast/the-founder-spartan-with-joe-de-sena/id1533716044?i=1000536808384

3

Becoming Available

Pain is inevitable. Suffering is optional.

– The Dalai Lama

MARATHON SEASON PROVIDED a gateway drug to a much bigger life purpose and assignment. The marathons showed me that I'm capable of much more than I ever realized physically, spiritually, and energetically. It also transformed my perspective: I began to look forward to challenges and massive goals, because it was no longer a question of whether I could accomplish it, but when. You see, the beautiful thing of putting yourself through hell voluntarily is that you cultivate grit, resilience, and an unshakable confidence. On the other side of pain is growth. These life lessons altered the way I began to see and show up in the world. For anyone who is currently struggling, suffering, or in a dark place, if you can see up, then you can get up. Then when you go through some adversity, you'll begin to develop a bulletproof mindset. If you didn't die, then you can make a comeback. The marathons were tough, hard as hell, and brutal, yet also the most beautiful and rewarding human experiment. I found myself in a place where I started to ponder if I could be successful at things that were not natural to me and that I lacked experience in. What kind of impact could I make if I became available for both my passion and my purpose in life? I still lacked clarity during this season but I was obsessed with both growth and the pursuit of identifying why I'm here. Spoiler alert: we are all here for a big reason.

January 2020, I set an intention and sent my best friend (also known as my brother Marc) a text. The text said something along the lines of "I'm available and I'm going to change my life this year and I don't know how but I know I'm here for a bigger purpose than where I'm currently floundering around . . ."

In March 2020, the pandemic surfaced, lockdown began, and I shut down my office for what I thought was going to be about two weeks tops. For the first time in my adult life, I found myself without an organized schedule and work-related purpose. I looked around and I observed that basically everybody I knew was watching *Tiger King* on Netflix and doing a hell of a lot of day drinking, which, without being

10

judgmental, I thought was a dangerous idea. My relationship with God had been growing rapidly for the past few years and I doubled down on my faith when I started my running journey. God and I communicated often, specifically during long runs.

I began to feel very called and intentional with this once-in-a-lifetime historic opportunity of extra time while the world stood still. I started tripling down on what I call "sharpening the axe." I was reading a lot and watching anything that could put me in the right frequency to receive creative and divine downloads. I was absolutely relentless in my pursuit of finding something bigger, more impactful, and important that also would give me happiness and fulfillment. One day it hit me like a nunchuck to the throat while I was thinking about what my actual passions and desires are in this world. Personal development is an obsession of mine. But what if it was more than a passion? What if it was a calling, my purpose, my assignment, and my contribution to the world?

I remember thinking I didn't want this lockdown to end because I was on to something. I asked myself what my gifts were. What was my superpower? What were my skill sets? Everyone has them. As clearly as God has ever communicated with me up until that point, I heard a whisper and it was revealed to me that I was, humbly, a very gifted communicator. I could move people. I could elevate peoples' spirits and infiltrate their souls. Now we were on to something, and I felt the most natural and exhilarating high of being alive and aligned. This was one of the most beautiful, important moments of my life up to this point. Now I knew I always had this in me but the truth of the matter is I was never available because I aligned myself with the wrong dream, surrounded by the wrong people with an unorganized avalanche of both empowering and limiting beliefs that needed structure and prioritization.

BANG! From studying personal development for years I cultivated a strategy to take my passion, personal development, and my gift of being an effective communicator and I married those two concepts. Of course, the writing has always been on the wall, but I needed to be available. Timing is everything. With the magic of thinking big and a newfound confidence and limitless belief system, creative divine downloads began flowing through my veins and heart like a waterfall at Niagara Falls. Personal development, upgrading identities, growth, and reinvention on the largest scale was my assignment. For the first time in my life I was truly available. Game on.

Ask Yourself: What are your skill sets or superpowers? Make a list.

4

Cultivate Lasting Symphony

It doesn't take time; it just takes alignment.

– Abraham Hicks

ON A RUN in Central Park during the pandemic, I received a download that nearly punched me in the teeth. I literally pulled over, paused my workout, and got to a beautiful park bench where a thought I had registered years prior still remained and came flying back at me like a boomerang. I remembered that I could purchase a domain on GoDaddy. Cultivate Lasting Symphony (CLS) was the brand name, a play on my initials Craig Landon Siegel, and it was a message that means to create a permanent growth-oriented and positive mentality. I had always loved the word *symphony* for many reasons; first because I'm strange, and second because I always thought that it was a beautiful word that illustrates an orchestra of sorts playing together in tempo. Did I mention that I'm weird and strange? I now embrace all of that and take pride in it.

CLS was born, and the clarity began to trickle in, drip by drip. CLS was going to become the future of personal development, sleek and classy and the face of positivity and reinvention. I had taken with me the power of thinking big and being available for only what could go right as opposed to what could go wrong and the momentum began to build. I was fired up and possessed a level of curiosity and drive that I had never quite experienced before. This was in alignment in a big way.

Later that day, I turned my iPhone camera on, hit video record and turned the device around to capture a short selfie of me proclaiming the mission statement of what CLS was to become. I imagined a 10-lane highway, with each lane consisting of a different way to make an impact: speaking, coaching, mentoring, a podcast, a book, a show, training, social media, and more. I built up about 20 seconds of courage that week and made another video reintroducing myself to the world of social media. I spoke to my tiny and adorable following of 300 Instagram followers and a Facebook presence that was on the rather small and not engaging side, so that viewers would have clarity on why I was

14

going to be posting about mindset and positivity using the initials CLS, as though I was on the verge of breaking the Internet and giving the world an injection of much needed faith, hope, and inspiration at a time when the world could really use it. If this was gonna hit, I'd have to make sure of one key character trait first.

Ask Yourself: What are you unsure of in your life right now? Instead of thinking about what could go wrong, make a list of all the possibilities of what could go right!

5

Raw Authenticity

The privilege of a lifetime is to become who you truly are.

– Joseph Campbell

THERE WAS ONLY one way this moonshot would hit and put a planet-size dent in the universe. I made a non-negotiable concrete commitment to myself that, for the first time in my life, I would show up as the 100% real, raw, authentic, weird, strange, and the unorthodox cat that I am, knowing with certainty, that I would not be everyone's cup of tea or glass of whiskey. No more people pleasing or trying not to ruffle feathers or any level of inauthenticity. The world would see me for who I am, all the great and the not so great. The right people would gravitate toward me, and the wrong people would part ways, and that would be okay. In fact, that would be preferred.

Here's the irony with this lesson: the more vulnerable I would show myself to be, the bigger the audience would grow and the thicker the connection with the community would be. As my friend, paralympic skier Amy Purdy,[1] and I discussed on an episode of *The CLS Experience*, vulnerability is both sexy and a superpower. Vulnerability displays courage. It showcases the ability to be brave and be seen without fear of judgment. Vulnerability illustrates power. If you're not afraid to show up naked, no one can hurt you or infiltrate your bubble of serenity. It reminds me of the ending of the movie *8 Mile* starring Eminem in which he elects to go first in the climactic rap battle, taking the initiative to show his cards, both the good and the bad, and own all his skeletons. That's true power.

An example of authenticity is someone who is full of self-love, magnetic, and owns every part of him- or herself. Being authentic is the key to an intimate connection for building rapport with your audience, customers, or life relationships in general. If you haven't been authentic up to this point, I challenge you right here right now to start being absolutely *you* and showing up to the world unapologetic about every part of you. There is only one of you. Not even identical twins have the same fingerprints, so don't try to be anyone else. Allow the world to see you for the beautiful and amazing person you were created to be.

Then, sit back and watch how the right people gravitate toward you while the wrong connections suddenly exit your life to your relief. Authenticity will create a life filter for you, bringing you closer to the people and experiences that are most aligned with the actual you, and distancing you from the wrong associations that no longer serve you. Thank me later.

Ask Yourself: How and where can you begin to show up more authentically?

Note

1. https://podcasts.apple.com/us/podcast/vulnerability-is-sexy-with-amy-purdy/id1533716044?i=1000566304817

6

The Three Rs: Redesign, Reenergize, and Reinvent

A vision without a strategy remains an illusion.

– Lee Bolman

Redesign

It was time to execute. But how do I get my mind right? How do I let go of all the limiting beliefs that no longer serve me? How do I boldly and confidently step into this new arena without any experience in the industry? This is where the Reinvention Formula was born. I created my 3R methodology. First and foremost we need to redesign our mindset.

Being enlightened is the key to understanding that we have a choice. We can decide which thoughts we allow to take up real estate inside our minds. Follow me here. Are you going to allow positive and productive thoughts to hold court in your mind to guide you, or will you be a prisoner and allow the negativity to spread like wildfire? Choose your hard: the pain of stepping into the unknown or the pain of regret wondering what could have happened if you stepped boldly into your dreams. What most people don't know is that just about 75% or more of our thoughts over the course of the day are actually negative. Don't take my word for it; this is backed by science. According to NeuroGym,[1] that my friend John Assaraf runs. He was a part of the global phenomenon book *The Secret* and he was also on the CLS Experience. So here's the billion-dollar question: How do the high achievers and world shakers block out that interference? Let's dive deeper.

First and foremost it begins with awareness. An absolute understanding that anytime you're vibrating on a lower frequency it is feedback from the universe telling you that your thoughts are not serving you. It's a green light to go in and do some redesigning. BANG! Time to replace the negative and disempowering thoughts with positive, constructive, and productive thoughts that will lead to brand-new, exciting, and empowering beliefs and self-love.

Now we are able to remove limitations and say goodbye to the imposter syndrome, or self-imposed self-doubt that we cultivated throughout life. Those experiences have been keeping us living inside a false reality or a self-imposed prison of the mind that limits us from achieving our best, which, to be clear, we were not born with. Now we are getting somewhere.

Here's the most impactful realization I've ever had the beautiful honor of discovering: thoughts are random, thinking is not. Let me run that back, and this is where you will want to whip out the highlighter. When we deliberately create new thoughts, new beliefs, and new behaviors, we begin to cultivate fresh and positive new dynamic results. We now have the power to redesign our mindset and create an exciting and limitless approach to making our thoughts work for us, not against us.

We've all heard that thoughts are things that have a frequency. Well, you better believe that's true! This is why you don't manifest what you want, you manifest what you are. So pay attention to the results life brings you. If you're not 100% in love with them, go back in and be super intentional with your thought process. Start by saying I can, I will, and I am worthy. Follow that up with I am here for a reason, I am unique, and I do absolutely have gifts to share with the world. Now take it from there and have fun creating a custom template of empowering thoughts to keep in your inventory thought box of magic, and play offense. From this very chapter, there is literally no excuse to ever turn a bad moment into a bad day ever again, because you can always transform from reactive to proactive by being purposeful and selective with your mindset and thought strategy. Your mindset can be your best friend or your worst enemy, but with the first of the three Rs at your disposal, you can now redesign any mindset that you desire and take back control of your life and what you'll create moving forward.

Reenergize

Anything worth doing in life requires a certain level of both passion and enthusiasm. This is where the second R comes into play. How do you get reenergized about something? You must absolutely identify your why. Why are you doing this in the first place, why is this important to you, why is this going to make an impact, why does the world need this? Take some time with this. Grab a journal, preferably a custom CLS one, of course! Write down why accomplishing these goals or dreams is important to you. Be specific and intentional here. When you have a strong and determined "why," you are able to push through the inevitable storms, challenges, and obstacles that are part of the process. On the flip side, when you do not have a strong purpose or "why" that energizes you, the first sign of adversity will cause you to crumble and submit to the pressure. You'd better negotiate the price of chasing your dreams in advance. Spoiler alert: sacrifice is par for the course. It's not likely, it's a guarantee. Now, I imagine you're asking yourself right about now what my purpose is that has me reenergized out of my mind. Let's dive in.

I spent 35 years on this planet searching for something more and bigger than myself. I had a lot of interesting stops on the journey that seemed like potential final destinations at the time. It was only through life experience and setbacks, poor choices, and dark seasons that I built a battle-tested bulletproof mindset through cultivating contrast. Contrast means you have experience with both the pretty and the ugly. The good and the bad. The champagne and the rock bottoms. Once I became available to identify my assignment, I was available for reinvention. Not just of my career, but my identity. I could be someone of impact, contribution, and purpose.

I want the world to know that reinvention is ready when you are. Period, end of story. It's never too late, you're never too old, there is literally no moment that can stop you from a season of reinvention as long as you believe in yourself and the process. The reinvention formula is for anyone who feels stuck, who thinks that it's too late, or who is seeking redemption and wants to change course and create a life of happiness, purpose, and fulfillment. That's my *why* and that is what has me reenergized.

Reinvent

We've now redesigned our mindset and created a new map or frame of how we will perceive both the world and ourselves moving forward. We now have tangible strategies in place to intentionally utilize positive and productive thoughts to change our beliefs. We have definitely and profoundly agreed to reorganize our mindset.

Additionally we have become reenergized about life and our new mission and purpose. We have momentum and a strong unbreakable "why" that fuels us like a fully charged battery that could light up all of Manhattan. It's called *purpose*. We lean into combining these two strategies and we're ready to reinvent ourselves to the world. Show up a little differently, think a little differently, think a little bigger, play bigger, be available, and take inspired action. Now we get to recreate ourselves by assuming a whole new upgraded identity. One that commands respect, attention, and never develops complacency or inauthenticity. We become the master of our own presence as opposed to letting others define that for us, as I did for so long. We utilize the three Rs and remake ourselves creating a volcano of new positive characteristics and assume the roles of artists working on our new identities like artists work on clay. We get to become symbols of people absolutely going for it, and living our lives purposely and intentionally.

For me, I wanted to create an overwhelming desire to believe in myself again, the way I began to in the beginning of lockdown during the pandemic. I don't think, I *know* that we are all here to leave our own unique mark. The third R is how we show up now, evolved, battle tested, and ready to level up and expect to receive blessings the same way we provide them. Reinvention isn't a feeling, it's a decision.

Since creating the methodology and applying the three Rs, CLS has taken the world by storm over the two years since its inception. We created one of the top business and self-help podcasts called *The CLS Experience*, which has featured the world's top entrepreneurs, business moguls, Hollywood actors, professional athletes, and celebrities who have achieved success in multiple industries. We have spoken and done workshops and executed keynote speeches all over the world, created a massive community including the CLS Membership and coached thousands of people on performance, business, and how to build a personal brand. The three Rs are a game changer and have helped facilitate a meteoric rise of the CLS brand and movement. Most importantly, it has provided the opportunity to change millions of lives and helped countless people while also creating a network for like-minded people to collaborate and support one another. Each R in the formula is as important as the others.

We need the tools to create a better mindset, the passion and energy to be congruent with our desires, and the action to show up, upgraded and reinvented, to showcase a more evolved and seasoned human, one who is magnetic and adds value. Reinvention is something we can all relate to in some capacity. It's the promise that positive change is one formula away from creating a totally new and upgraded life.

Ask Yourself: Which limiting beliefs that are currently holding you back can you challenge right now?

Note

1. https://blog.myneurogym.com/new-study-you-have-6900-thoughts-a-day-dont-make-yours-negative

7

Gaining Clarity

Clarity is the moment we see without opening our eyes.

– Stephanie Banks

I COULD ALREADY sense all the eye rolling. But how, Craig? How do I get clarity, how do I identify my why, how do I locate my purpose? If you absolutely have no idea what your passions are, you can begin to make a list of your skill sets. Trust me, we all have skills. What are you good at? What can you help someone with? After writing down what we love and or what we're good at, we begin to formulate a path.

If you're still reading this and scratching your head thinking that you have no interests or skills then here is my suggestion. Reach out to 5–10 people who know you best and ask them, straight up, what they think you like and are good at. Trust me, once you collect the data, there will be some commonalities, and we can go from there. I don't care if you love plants or reviewing movies or insects, if you're willing to be available and hustle, you will create opportunities to monetize. I can't be convinced otherwise. It's just an energetic exchange of your passion behind an idea and people willing to pay you to help them with it or hear you speak about it.

Please understand that if you're one of those people who really finds it challenging to gain clarity, then maximum effort on your end is required to journal, white board, or ask your friends for data to get momentum here. Sometimes just identifying what you don't like is progress in itself. In addition, please buy into the power of journaling and white boarding and use them just as an overall brain dump. These creative techniques have made all the difference for me when putting the vision together for CLS and they provided the DNA for the Reinvention Formula.

To be sure we cover every route in our pursuit to getting clear on our vision, it's important that we acknowledge that clarity follows action. You have to be willing to try new things, look silly, or throw some spaghetti at the wall to see what feels good or what doesn't. If you think that by modeling a monk, sitting Indian style and meditating, you will automatically gain a jolt of awareness and an exact direction to take, you may be fooling yourself. Sometimes you have to cultivate that 20 seconds of courage, apply for that acting class, or take public speaking lessons, try entrepreneurship, or even approach that intriguing stranger and put yourself out there. You have to step into the arena. Become a gladiator and cultivate the mindset and have fun with the journey. Clarity is on the other side of uncomfortable action.

Ask Yourself: What inspired action can you take right now that will be followed up with clarity?

8

Personal Branding

Everything you are, say, and do represents your brand.

— *Author unknown*

WHEN I SET the intention to begin CLS, I realized I had a lot of work and strategizing ahead of me in order to make the world-shaking impact I had in mind. Although I had been a relatively private introvert to this point with a whopping three hundred Instagram followers and a small Facebook network, I was aware of the world we live in. The power of social media, being able to connect with anyone in any capacity, utilizing the social-media juggernaut to optimize marketing strategies and put myself out there—this was definitely uncomfortable for me at the time. However, I also knew that the real growth I needed was waiting on the other side of messy and uncomfortable action.

I began to brand myself as CLS and create content consisting of motivational videos with tangible strategies. I remember thinking how important it was to begin to think of myself as a brand moving forward and have the mindset that the camera is always on. I began to become super intentional and calculated with everything I posted.

The world of social media has provided such an amazing opportunity to market yourself and extend your reach, if done correctly. Your brand is a frequency. It has a pulse, an energy, and it provides a feeling. It's the same way when you think about Nike, Apple, Disney, Rolex, Chanel, or a person like Tony Robbins or Tom Brady; you get a feeling from the vibe that that brand or person portrays. Apple may create a feeling of the market leader for technology, and Disney may make you think of family movies or theme parks. Tony Robbins most likely makes you think of personal development, and Tom Brady creates a feeling of championships and football.

I was excited by the possibility of creating a brand that would be identified with growth, self-development, reinvention, great collaborations, and community. I could add to the brand as we grew and figured things out along the way, but it was important to have a vibe that we were going for. I highly recommend having fun with this but also being intentional and strategic. A brand is like the modern-day term for a reputation. You can build it to your liking, but you can also ruin it with poor choices and associations. Be selective with how you show up and who you surround yourself with if you want to gain recognition, respect, and credibility.

Let's pull back the curtain on how to create your brand and how to create a vision. A great strategy that I utilized here was creating a personal-brand vision board. I suggest selecting images that represent you, your interests, and your brand aspirations. Have fun and be authentic here. Mount the images on a physical board or use a moodboard or scrapbook. (For those of you asking what in the world a moodboard is, let me explain. It's a collection of images, colors, and fonts that perfectly define what a project is about.) Observe the overall themes and stories that emerge here, and create an outline of your brand narrative based on your observations. A story will begin to emerge and guide you in a direction. This is an invaluable strategy to create something that feels personal, authentic, and in alignment with the person you are and will be continuing to grow into.

It's time to define your superpowers. Spoiler alert, we all have them. Brainstorm your strongest skills. Now let's think about how these skills could translate into personal brand success. How can you use these to elevate and promote your brand? Now that the creative juices are flowing, it's time to think about what you want your brand to be. What is your direction? Who do you want to talk to? Who is your audience? What are your social media platforms? Next, let's map out where we want our message to be felt and seen. For instance, when you think of Disney, you most likely think of joy, happiness, cartoons and a family-oriented vibe. In my case, I wanted CLS to be perceived as the Apple of personal development—sleek, quality, and always leveling up. The clarity should be hitting you now like a shot of espresso and you should be feeling creative, abundant, and in synergistic alignment with the direction of your brand and the future impact.

Once the frequency has taken shape and the very thought of your brand has a vibe, it's time to consider forming brand collaborations. This has many layers to it. You may want to consider who you would like to collaborate with to share audiences or to begin to form a certain standard for how people will associate your brand. For example, for me the *CLS Experience* podcast was going to be massive and the guests that the audience would expect to hear from were of the highest standard. I was very intentional and committed to that even from the very beginning. Another layer of collaboration is potential future partnerships or sponsorships. Another example is the *CLS Experience* podcast being sponsored by *Shark Tank*'s billionaire Mark Cuban's brand, Three Commas. When you think of Mark Cuban, you think of a great businessman and entrepreneur. That's a strategic partnership that feels in alignment with who we are and what we represent. Be very selective and strategic with anyone that you are going to associate with, because people will create a belief one way or the other, so you might as well hold yourself to a very high standard here.

The last part of branding that was critical for me to pay close attention to was the look of the branding. Whether it was our CLS logo, the colors of our posts, or the energy in our video's and speeches, I wanted to create something that felt good to me and most importantly was authentic. You have to be authentic, genuine, and create something that is refreshing. Let's face it, many markets or industries have become saturated. There is a lot of noise out there. However, as I always say, there is always room for the best. I'm very visual and I like certain colors. I gravitated toward Instagram a lot because of the visual creative landscape. When you go to our Instagram feed you'll see very intentional coloring and energy which creates a vibe. Remember, you are the vibe! Now, although I understand not everyone reading this is branding themselves, in the world we live in today, thinking of yourself as a brand can only be advantageous and help you create a life of impact, passion, and intention while also allowing you to extend your reach and thus make the biggest dent in the universe. If you have no aspirations to put yourself out there or lean into entrepreneurship or allow yourself to be seen, that's okay too. However, if you're reading this book, then there's a very good chance that this can benefit you and get you started with clarity and intention and set forth a path toward alignment and making your mark on the world.

Ask Yourself: What vibe do you want your brand to project outward? How do you want people to feel about you or your brand when they think of you?

9

Messy Action

If you're not embarrassed by who you were a year ago, you're probably not growing enough.

– Chris Voss

THE MOST IMPORTANT factor in preparing to reinvent yourself and fulfill your assignment here in life is to not be afraid to look silly along the way, especially in the beginning stages. If you've made it this far into this book I think it's safe to say that you're not just interested in reinvention, you're committed. This means that you will not be everyone's cup of tea or shot of tequila, and that's okay. If you worry about what other people think of you, like I did for the first 35 years of my life, then you'll never get off the ground. You have to lean into messy action. *Done* will always be better than *perfect*.

When I look back at some of the first pieces of content that I created when I first started CLS, I can't help but laugh. I have come such a long way. To give an analogy, it's like going back to your favorite television show and watching the pilot episode from season one. It has that vibe that seems as if the producers didn't know for certain if the show would get renewed for season two, and it has that smaller-budget feel. This is not only normal, but is exactly how it should feel when you first begin. Then you stay the course, you gain experience, and you continue to beat on your craft, creating a much more seasoned and tested product. You absolutely have to have a sense of humor and not take yourself too seriously. The greatest icons and world shakers have never been afraid to look silly, to take messy action, and to even fail a few times before they got it right. This is all a part of the process. This is why I love to say marry the process and divorce from the outcome. Fall in love with taking action and fully acknowledge and embrace that it's a journey and you will continue to improve, grow, and come into your own.

Changing my perspective from being a recovering perfectionist to someone who takes pride in stepping into the arena regardless of how much experience I have has helped me quantum leap in all areas of my life—business and marathon running and everything in between. The real victory and joy is in the pursuit and the journey, not the final destination. I love to look back on my content from even three months ago, and have a good laugh at how much I've grown since. At the end of the day, we have to have fun. And here's a reality: none of us make it out of this human experience alive. Aside from making a massive impact and contribution, unapologetically making a ton of money, and falling in love, we must have fun and not take each activity too seriously or we will always be waiting for that perfect time to begin.

From my life experience I can assure you that there will never be the perfect time to start; you have to be willing to look silly and step into the arena. We figure things out along the way and we gain wisdom. Although I am not a parent yet, everyone I know that is can confirm that there is never a perfect time to become one, but you figure it out. It's the same with reinvention. One hundred percent of the things you do now, get done. Begin. Take your shot. Anyone that takes big swings at life is also prepared to take big misses along the way. It's a part of the process and is your best feedback and teacher. Bottom line: be that gladiator and step inside the arena and we will figure out the rest along the way. No one has ever regretted trying something new that they were passionate about, but on the flip side everyone I know later in life always regrets not showing up, not taking that shot, and not pursuing something they were passionate about due to a fear of failure or looking silly. As my friend Amy Porterfield[1] said on *The CLS Experience*, "You have to get in the game." You can't win from sitting on the sidelines. Get your hands dirty and enter the arena.

Ask Yourself: What messy action can you take right now without worrying about being perfect?

Note

1. https://podcasts.apple.com/us/podcast/get-in-the-game-with-amy-porterfield/id1533716044?i=1000587037101

10

Adversity

Sometimes we have to taste the darkness to want to see the light.

— Craig Siegel

IN CASE YOU needed a reminder, adversity is a part of life. In fact, obstacles and setbacks are inevitable on the journey. Just when you think you have it all figured out, you'll get punched in the gut and brought to your knees. You'll taste blood, defeat, and sadness just to name a few. Here's the paradigm shift though. When you decide that life happens for you and not to you, now you realize that all the tough blows are really a higher power's way of protecting and propelling you to something much greater. With this mindset you can never be crippled by disappointment because you know that whatever has caught you off guard and seems like a setback is just a detour to something much more in alignment for you.

That's the key: it's *for* you and not *to* you. We are never a victim. Trust me, I used to love to play victim—why me, great things never happen for me, and so forth. That mentality is a choice. Then I doubled down on the inner work and I came up with another option during tough seasons of life. Another choice is the victor mentality, which says try me, adversity. Bring it on. On the other side of this pain is massive growth. I may not be able to identify it right now but as the iconic late Steve Jobs once said, you can never connect the dots looking forward, only backward. So trust the process and maintain that being-protected aura, and you'll never be truly crushed.

In 2021 I was at a speaking engagement where I tasted a nice serving of adversity and humble pie. You know the kind of curveball when you're expecting a fastball that totally throws you for a loop. The day before I was scheduled to perform my keynote speech, I, against my usual sense of risk management (especially considering I was training for the Chicago Marathon) found myself playing barefoot beach football with the company's employees. It seemed like a good idea at the time. Now, looking back, I was guided to participate and you're about to find out why. The owner of the company dropped back and threw a dart of a pass to the left side of the beachy field, where I sprinted to catch the ball in stride and score a touchdown. When I caught the pass

I stepped down hard on a very flat section of the sand that felt more like concrete. I thought for sure I had broken my foot. I remember having no time to rest or really check it out, because we had dinner plans and the next morning I would be delivering my workshop. I couldn't believe the throbbing pain I felt. The next morning at the event, I asked the catering hall for some ice and sat in the back and rested my foot on the cold ice searching desperately for some relief. I put on my shoe, delivered the presentation and hopped on a plane a day later and back home to the Big Apple. Immediately I searched for a doctor in my network who could take an X-ray and get this injury diagnosed properly so I could begin the road to recovery and potentially still have a shot at the Chicago Marathon. Doctor visit booked, and off I go to jump on this thing and be proactive. X-ray comes back negative and the doctor diagnoses me with a sprained ligament and gives me this big bulky black boot to wear for four to six weeks and after that I should be healed and good to go. A couple weeks go by and this foot injury begins to worsen. I pride myself in being able to handle pain very well, I have a high tolerance, but something seemed off here. My girlfriend at that time and now fiancée, Olesya—who was suffering PTSD from seeing me in this boot caused by her memory of when she was in the same boot a year before I met her—said she thought I should get an MRI just in case. Interestingly enough I was having the same intuition. I called the doctor to request one despite him thinking it was unnecessary. The lesson here: always listen to your intuition and always get a second opinion.

I can never forget this moment. I was upstairs at my New York City apartment gym using the exercise bicycle and I don't mean the trendy Peloton. I was using a stationary bike with this big clunky annoying boot on when I received a phone call from the doctor's assistant. "Hey Craig, we're going to need you to come in," he said with a low-vibe disempowering tone that felt like something not positive was going to be the conclusion here. I said, "I have a packed schedule, so kindly just hit me with the update. Is it torn?" I asked. The doctor's assistant stuck by his guns and reiterated that they need me to come back in. I got a little frustrated here and said with a sarcastic tone "I don't have time to come back just tell me what's up, is it torn and what are the next steps?" After putting me on a brief hold the doctor now on the line

said, "Craig, actually the ligament looks good, no concerns there." I
said, "Okay, great. Then what's the issue? I'll never forget the doctor
responding with a low and surprised tonality that portrayed an unnerv-
ing sense of anxiousness, "We found a very rare tumor at the bottom of
your foot, and it could potentially be cancerous as well."

Ask Yourself: What current obstacle can become a blessing in disguise with a reframe?

11

The Paradigm Shift

Your perspective will either become your prison or your passport.
                                                  – *Steven Furtick*

THE OLD CRAIG would have showered in guilt, shame, and self-pity and moaned about this happening to me. The reinvented Craig knew that this was a blessing in disguise, and, although I have no idea why, I would one day look back and realize this happened *for* me. Maybe I needed to slow down as I had been going 100 miles per hour with CLS up until this point. I gave myself grace and allowed myself to feel all the feels for the rest of that day. My fiancée and mom proceeded to Google the rare tumor and as it turns out it could be a serious issue if not treated quickly.

I think it's important here to illustrate the power of giving yourself the grace to be sad and disappointed. Take that moment and approach it how you see fit; however, make that unwavering commitment that the very next day it's on to strategies, tactics, and cultivating a game plan and a list of doctors and surgeons to visit to collect some data. And so I did. I scheduled three doctor appointments over the next five days and began to take inventory of what we were dealing with here and what were the necessary next steps. It was during this season that I also began to be very open and transparent with my rapidly growing audience. I started a new show on Instagram called transparency hour in which I'd go on and talk about real-life challenges and how we handle them. I hoped this would open the space for tough conversations to be had to inspire others that they are not alone. The more I openly spoke about this tumor situation, which until that point was uncharacteristic of me, the deeper the connection grew with my community.

There is real power in vulnerability and exposing the tough parts of life as well. One of the greatest things a leader can do is to show up even when things aren't all rainbows and butterflies and stay strong in the face of adversity. My openness about my tumor did two things at once. It exploded the CLS community and it gave me confidence and courage to continue to open the space for tough conversations. The world needs more tough conversations about the challenging times. I take pride in creating space both on the *CLS Experience* podcast and on my shows to show up authentically, with no armor, and talk about the rotten situations. Having a tumor in my foot, although it provided me the opportunity to slow down and do some much-needed extra inner and energy work, was still a bad situation. I gained so much wisdom and courage during this season by showing up and being vulnerable about the fact that I don't know for sure what will happen next with regard to cancer and so forth. But I know it's all going to work out one way or the other, and I am here to deal with it gracefully and with a positive and optimistic attitude. That is something we can all do during crappy times and unexpected life situations—show up regardless and showcase a bulletproof mindset. Just to be clear here, this doesn't mean that we're not hurting inside; what it means is that we're not victims and were not prisoners of circumstance. I also encourage you to exercise your faith here. Don't just *think* or *believe*, but feel that it will all work out for the best.

After interviewing the three best doctors in Manhattan who I believed to be most qualified for this surgery, I felt guided and made my choice. I felt a sense of calm and trust throughout this entire process from diagnosis to the doctor selection and up until the day of surgery. I have really worked on and grown my relationship with God over the past decade, but I have really doubled down on that dynamic since the pandemic. When you have a belief in something bigger than yourself, something perhaps even supernatural, you feel comfort in surrendering to the process and trusting that the outcome will be in your best interest. This whole season was very interesting and eye opening to me. I can't stress enough how much Craig 1.0 would have felt sorry for himself during this experience. Glad that I have committed to the inner game to transform from reactive to proactive and set my intentions and then be and allow. Surgery went great, I emerged with a hole in my foot that required stitches and crutches and some unusual down time with no fitness for at least the next four to six weeks—or so it was suggested. I remember being instructed how to properly utilize the crutches at the hospital and my only thought was that I would become a master of recovery.

The first 24 hours after surgery was a tough pill to swallow. The very next morning while getting acclimated to my updated situation, having to hop out of bed to grab my crutches and propel myself to the kitchen, I received a phone call from my dad. It's interesting how you can hear a phone ring and automatically know the news about to hit will be troublesome. "Hi Craig, we have some upsetting news to report to you." Is everything okay, Dad? What's up? "We have to put the family dog down today." The dog I got myself in college who was with my family for 16-plus years and was absolutely a part of the family, as anyone with a dog can confirm, had not been herself. She had many health issues for about a year and had ultimately had enough. I know this will sound controversial, and although I was still coming off from the anesthesia from the prior day's surgery, I felt sad but also a bit relieved. Maki had been suffering for a bit now and it was time for her to cross the rainbow bridge as they say and be relieved of her pain. This was still during the pandemic, and there were no vets available, so we had one come to the house. My brother picked me up from Manhattan to shoot out to Long Island on crutches to be with my family. This whole experience was actually quite spiritual and as beautiful as it possibly could be, as Maki was put down in my mother's arms while we all said goodbye and I spent her final moments with her in her home. Talk about very challenging back-to-back days for me, from tumor surgery to putting my dog down. I remember thinking that what I wanted was to show up for our CLS membership call the next day because the CLS community lights me up like a Christmas tree. That's the beauty of becoming aligned and creating a life you love with a career you're in love with. In the toughest of moments, you want to work because your work isn't really work; it fills your cup. One of the secret cheat codes to life is to identify your passions and turn it into your purpose by building a life around what you love. I remember hearing all the time when I was younger that if you love what you do for a living, you will never work a day in your life. I used to be so skeptical of that as I believed there is no such thing as loving your work. I thought it would always feel like a J-O-B. Boy, am I grateful to have been wrong about that one!

With physical fitness—which is nonnegotiable for me now—removed from my schedule, I decided to take that time and energy and double down on my mental fitness. After all, it is my career now. I had always been skeptical of quantum teachings and all the invisible infinite energy fields of abundance because I was so stubborn. I figured if it was beyond my senses, then I couldn't buy in. But then, I put my ego aside, acknowledged that I didn't know what I didn't know, and returned to a book I had read years prior called *The Secret,* which is all about the law of attraction. As of the writing of this book, many of the stars of the movies and authors of the book have become friends of mine, and they have appeared on the *CLS Experience* podcast. To say I surrendered to these concepts and bought in could quite possibly be the understatement of the century. I entered the quantum (see Chapter 12) while recovering from surgery and I haven't left since. This is when I truly became a magnet for abundance, and the blessings began to swarm toward me like bees to nectar. Surrender and flow.

Ask Yourself: Which perspective can you look at from a different angle?

12

Into the Quantum

The universe doesn't hear what you are saying, it only feels the vibration of what you are offering.

– Abraham Hicks

I FIND IT fascinating that you could read a book in different seasons of your life and have a totally different experience with the work. I had read *The Secret* years prior and took some nuggets from it, but the truth is I wasn't fully available to receive all it offered. The law of attraction has become a bit controversial in recent years. Some people say that book was incomplete because it leaves out the law of GOYA, also known as get off your ass. In other words, aside from setting your intention, one must also do the work, put in the reps, and get after it. I think that's fair. Once you create an idea, something becomes a possibility. When you follow that with inspired action, now that idea becomes a probability.

Here's my interpretation of the quantum field also known as the infinite possibilities of energy or the vortex. This is a vibrational universe. In other words, we don't manifest what we want, we manifest what we are. The reason this is so powerful is because, if you're not absolutely loving the results you're getting from the universe, it's feedback that your current frequency or your vibe is low and as a result you're attracting low vibe type of results.

This has been the biggest breakthrough for me. Now I go back in and apply The Reinvention Formula and start being super intentional with my thoughts to create empowering beliefs, and now I can operate from a state of bliss or a high vibration. As a result, I become a magnet for all the abundance out there. Here's the thing, we don't need to create the market out there for the amazing creative ideas, or all the money we unapologetically want, or anything we desire for that matter. The market already exists. It's our job to raise our hand and claim it and show up available and magnetic and be a container for it.

Let me break it down further. Do you ever wake up absolutely on fire, as though you can't be stopped? You find yourself at the right place, at the right time, with great ideas gravitating toward you? For instance, you're on a sales call and you have the perfect rebuttal for every objection, or you're at an event or social gathering and not afraid to approach and open a conversation with anyone with no hesitation. That's when you're in a really high vibe state. Things begin to slow down for you and you just see the whole chessboard of life. Like a great NFL quarterback in the fourth quarter; when most feel the pressure, but the high vibe elite quarterback (perhaps Tom Brady) sees the whole field in front of him and can anticipate all the defenders' intentions and as a result throws the perfect pass and wins the game. What if you could tap into your toolbox and utilize key principles to stay in this frequency for a full day? A full week? A month—perhaps forever? It wouldn't be what you could accomplish. It would be more like what could you not accomplish. From a guy who was always about mindset and NLP (neuro-linguistic programming), this energy stuff totally accelerated my growth. Let's pull back the curtain even more here.

When you raise your own energy, people and things will naturally become attracted to you. You see, everything is energy. This energy travels in frequencies and vibrations, and knowing that, we can begin to understand that every thought and even every intention carries its own energy. When you state an intention out loud, that very thought energy vibrates within the cells of your body and sends an extremely powerful message to your subconscious mind. This is why each and every thought will either empower you or on the contrary, disempower you. I can't stress this enough: you must be very strategic with the thoughts you allow to hang out inside your mind.

It is true that thoughts are random, but thinking is not. So while we only have limited control over our thoughts throughout the day, we can take full control in choosing a new thought. One that elevates us and makes us feel enthusiastic and empowered. This stuff right here, is the meat and potatoes of how to stay high vibe or in that superelevated frequency when you constantly feel on fire and the world seems to provide you with the blissful manifestations you desire. So, knowing this now, if you change the vibrational energy you put out into the world, you create a completely different world, because again, this is a vibrational universe.

Double down on this chapter of the book. Reread it until it makes sense and you can apply it to your life. Go absolutely crazy with the highlighter here. You are the vibe and you are the frequency, and you get to choose what you're tuned into. Will you decide to tune into abundance, the limitless energy field, and the quantum where time stands still and you can create anything you desire? Or will you choose to tune into scarcity and the world of not enough? Choose wisely.

Now I can already hear the questions from this chapter. How do you make this information more easily accessible and digestible? The more you practice choosing empowering thoughts to create a state of high consciousness or high vibe, the longer you can sustain this frequency. How do you stay in this state? You must create systems in place to block out all the potential interference. You know: that scarcity mindset we cultivated from growing up with poor money stories or the negative self-talk or even people who give off negative energy. When these stories or negative self-talk begin to show up, you must make a commitment to not be available to entertain them. Instead choose what you are available for such as all the prosperity and abundance out there that you would like to attract into your life.

Awareness here is the key. You can't change it if you can't see it. Pay attention to why you're feeling certain ways and then choose to strategically replace disempowering thoughts or stories with new fresh blissful abundant ones. Go for it, and set your intention to attract unlimited abundance. Become in harmony with your intention and stay blissful.

Ask Yourself: How can you elevate your vibration right now?

13

From Tumor to the NYC Marathon

Nothing is impossible, the word itself says I'm possible!

— Audrey Hepburn

LOOKING BACK ON this whole season it's obvious that the foot injury was divine intervention. I needed to slow down and begin to practice my feminine energy to go hand-in-hand with my masculine energy. In other words up until this point I had been on my grind. That hardest worker in the room mentality that was always do, do, do and go, go, go until it came to a head. I needed to begin to tap into this quantum field of intention and limitless abundance and begin to allow and to be. While there is always a need for the season of grind, it is not sustainable. This invisible energy stuff really captivated me and I began to operate from a whole new more powerful frequency. Instead of just thinking or believing in things to happen, I began to feel them happening.

Although the Chicago Marathon was now off the table due to the fact that I still had a hole in my foot with stitches as it continued to heal, I began to allow creative divine downloads to come through me. I started to think of the possibility of signing up for the TCS NYC Marathon, which would give me three extra weeks to heal and potentially have the stitches removed, giving me an at-bat or a crack at that thing. Now, the difference between this possibility and the reason I wanted to run the Chicago Marathon were complete opposites. Chicago was ego driven, because I wanted to run to hit a certain goal and make myself feel good about that. I think it's productive to have audacious personal goals but as you evolve and become more enlightened, you begin to realize what's really important and what's not. Hitting a new PR (or personal record or best, as they say in the running world) is great and always a good feeling, but the path I'm now heading toward is much more important than personal goals and wants.

In order to enter the NYC Marathon this late in the season I would have to sign up for a charity and raise money. Of course, the American Cancer Society came to me instantly, and the opportunity to both raise money to help advancements to battle public enemy number one (cancer), and also inspire and elevate the spirit of my best friend (also known as my dad) would be much bigger than me or any personal ego-driven goal I could ever accomplish.

With every hour that passed I began to feel stronger and more aligned with this intention. We've already established that intention is infinite potential, activating our physical and nonphysical appearance here on this earth, and so my thought process was—as I continued to stay tapped into this quantum field—I am formless energy. In fact I began to realize that I am a soul and a spirit having a human experience. This five-foot-seven-inch vessel (who is kinda handsome, maybe not, depending on your taste) is the vehicle for my human experience that contains my soul and spirit, which is abundant and limitless. What transpired next was the biggest spiritual awakening yet for me.

Day by day as we got closer to the NYC Marathon I began to feel the power of running visually and spiritually, and inspiring my dad to keep fighting his battle. I wanted to do my part in contributing to the American Cancer Society, and the idea of removing my personal desires and replacing them with much bigger, more important and impactful desires captivated me in a beautiful and spiritual way I had never quite experienced before. Intention set. With my appointment coming up with the doctor to get the stitches removed, I was getting ready emotionally to run this thing tapped into the quantum. Simple, right? Bring on some more adversity please with a side of obstacles.

I got to the doctor jazzed, enthusiastic, and inspired to get the stitches out. He very methodically unwrapped my foot and took a good, nice two-minute look at my foot without saying a word. My frequency went from a solid 10 to about a 7 as I could feel something was off. Then it dipped below a 5 as I eagerly anticipated the doctor's unexpected update. Then I took a moment to myself and instructed myself that no matter what news was about to come my way, it was all happening for me and it was all going to work out even better than I imagined. Bring it on, Doc.

As it turns out, due to the fact that the bottom of my foot was so sensitive and constantly being used, the doctor suggested we keep the stitches in for another two weeks to be cautious and ensure that it healed properly. This would make the NYC Marathon a very close call. In fact, any type of physical training was out of the cards at this point. If this was going to work, it was going to be all mindset and quantum. Just the way I like it. Challenge accepted. Marathon booked, and all I really wanted was a crack at this thing by getting to the starting line, totally releasing any sort of expectations other than raising money to battle cancer and inspiring my dad.

The truth is I am trying to be very humble here, but I felt this sense of calm and an inner confidence that I have never quite felt before. Knowing that the tumor was not cancerous and that life happens *for* us—this was all a part of God's plan. I needed to shed my ego, learn the quantum, and have a stage to inspire millions of people in the CLS community, as well as my dad, who could really use some extra inspiration at a time when, as we all know, cancer can be quite taxing on your mindset in addition to your body. The table was set and the NYC Marathon was on the menu. All I needed to do was tap into the infinite energy field of possibilities knowing with absolute certainty that I am a soul and a spirit having a human experience and that this five-foot-seven-inch vessel would hold up, one foot and all. Not that it mattered, but the idea of running a PR with zero physical training for 26.2 miles of the iconic five boroughs at a second opportunity for the greatest marathon in the world sounded and felt like a storybook ending with a side order of redemption from my first marathon, when I failed to break the four-hour benchmark. Just writing this chapter gives me the chills.

This is real life at its finest. When you start to believe in yourself and you're available for life's abundance, you get to a frequency where you no longer just think and believe that things will work out. You begin to feel it almost like shape shifting your manifestations to fruition. This life moment for me was pivotal in that I had turned a corner and really leveled up with my inner game. I was so intentional with my thoughts here that my beliefs began to become so strong and powerful that I felt the whole race happening for me in a cinematic-like beautiful symphony of bliss and emotion through visualization. This whole experience was magical and I was excited for the opportunity.

Stepping into the arena of the concrete jungle for a second time, this time with no physical training as preparation, which was replaced by a wild spiritual journey that really picked up steam after the tumor diagnosis when I dove head first into the Secret and all the quantum content I could consume, I felt a bizarre sense of tranquility and peace. I had made it to the starting line, which was the big win here and the most important task at hand. Now, I just needed to surrender and flow. There's nothing stronger than the human spirit on fire. My soul was lit.

This whole race was an otherworldly experience. I remember flying through the first half with no indication that I had not been able to train physically nor any sign of rust. I think running a marathon in general is significantly more mental than physical. People may disagree, but this experience proved otherwise. One of the most beautiful and emotional experiences in life for me is on mile 16, when you enter Manhattan off a quiet and creepy bridge full of silence and footsteps, and then you're swarmed with the cheers of the crowd as you make that left onto first avenue. They call this thunder alley, and you can literally feel the ground shaking as millions of spectators await the runners with cheers, screaming, and encouragement. My family and friends were hanging out on the left-hand side of First Avenue at about 70th Street, where I located them, ran over to them, kissed Olesya, hugged my brother, and then took off to complete the rest of the 26.2 mile beast. Not only did I survive this day, but I thrived with a new personal best time (at that time) of 3:39:29 and, most importantly, inspired my dad, the loyal and rapidly growing CLS community, and made a contribution to the forever fight against public enemy number one, cancer. What a moment!

There were some consequences, because anything magical and special usually comes with sacrifice. I broke my foot somewhere during the run, as I would find out a week later after getting an MRI as a precaution to ensure that the cells of the tumor were not reemerging. I also ended up in the emergency room right after the race to get my toe drained as I had formed the biggest blister I had ever seen that consumed my entire toe. All that being said, it was worth every moment, all the blood, sweat, and tears, and this marathon experience was something I will never forget. In fact, just writing about it right now has me tearing up. It was an absolutely beautiful and complete spiritual experience. Based on this result alone, I cannot be convinced that running isn't mostly mental.

The biggest takeaway from this was how impactful it is when you do something for a much bigger cause than to appease your own individual wants and desires. This mindset to make an impact and inspire others would become the primary reason that I do anything moving forward. There is no better feeling than elevating others with your own actions. Am I proud of that PR? Absolutely! But it doesn't compare to how happy I was to elevate my dad's spirits to continue his battle and keep on fighting. Absolutely priceless! Although the story arc from tumor diagnosis to the NYC Marathon finish line concluded one particular story arc, the real journey had only just begun. Tapping into this infinite possibility energy field of potential and abundance was where I would live for the rest of my life. This is where the momentum really began to mount.

Ask Yourself: What's a bigger purpose that you can tap into that's meaningful and significant to you?

14

Upgrading Your Identity

Becoming the best version of yourself requires you to continuously edit your beliefs, and to upgrade and expand your identity.

– James Clear

THE MOST IMPORTANT factor to your reinvention isn't what you think it is. The big pivot or career change is the byproduct of the upgrade to your identity. You hear many thought leaders talk about raising your thermostat or their container for what they believe to be possible for them. This concept is the difference that makes the difference. You cannot outgrow your own self-worth.

I'd like to ask you some powerful questions right now. Let's be radically honest with each other right now because there has to be awareness in order to totally transform and reinvent yourself. Do you believe you are worthy of success? Do you believe there is a field of limitless abundance out there waiting for you to tap into? Do you believe there's more than enough to go around—the happiness, the fulfillment, the money, love, and all the meaningful relationships? I promise you there is.

You have to be available for it and call it into your life, but first you have to change the stories you've been telling yourself for years. The belief that there is not enough is a scarcity mindset and will get you nowhere fast. What do you honestly think is the big difference between people who go on to create a life full of abundance and the people who accept mediocrity? It's the beliefs that they possess. Now, if you've made it this far into *The Reinvention Formula*, then you have already declared that you were committed to the teachings, strategies, and lessons, so now it's time to level up your thinking.

Begin to think of yourself as a magnet. Like attracts like. You become what you think about most, so if you continue to go on thinking that you're not enough and that there isn't enough, what do you think you're going to attract into your life? The same things! Why? Because your thoughts are things, they have a frequency, so right about now is a great time to start thinking that you are worthy of being a massive magnet for success. See yourself living in abundance and you will attract it. Most people subconsciously think about what they don't

60

want, and then they feel sorry for themselves when they continue to attract those results. In order to upgrade your identity and what's possible for you, you have to focus on what can go right for you and double down on how valuable you truly are to this world.

When you really begin to understand this and apply it, you begin to enhance your identity. You begin to expect abundance and positive developments to transpire in your life. From the upgraded identity, you begin to show up differently in the world. You raise your vibration and become a match for great things to happen. Just to be clear, on a lower vibration you are a match as well, but only for the lower undesirable results that you don't want. You are the vibe! Feel it, own it, and show up accordingly.

One of my favorite movies that has made a strong impact on my mindset is *The Matrix*. There are so many lessons in this film, but one specifically that stands out for this chapter is this: When Morpheus is training Neo to understand his potential to fulfill the prophecy of him being "the one," he tells Neo that there is a big difference between knowing the path and walking the path. Let that one really sink in here. There is a scene where they are sparring inside a dojo and Morpheus tells Neo that he's stronger than how he is currently performing, but Neo needs to not *think* he is, but *know* he is.

I have goosebumps just thinking about how powerful this is for our lives. This is not to be confused with arrogance. There is a monster difference between cockiness and confidence. On our record-breaking podcast *The CLS Experience*, I begin every conversation by asking the guest what their superpower is. I love to get a feel for the legends and what makes them tick. I'm fascinated with dissecting what makes the greats so dynamic. What actually separates them from the rest.

I think one of my biggest superpowers is my concrete and bulletproof self-belief that I have cultivated by applying the principles in this book. The biggest shift I had in my life was when I gave birth to the Three Rs during the pandemic and I had to get real honest with myself about choosing different thoughts and eliminating all the negative beliefs and stories I had been replaying subconsciously in my mind.

Why not you? You absolutely do have a message, and the world will be better for you owning it and stepping into your power. This commit-ment to releasing all the bullshit you've been telling yourself about why you are not worthy is the first step toward upgrading your identity. Then, you begin to think, feel, and act differently. You can begin to show up with a little swag, an aura, a vibe that portrays that you are feeling yourself. There's nothing more attractive than someone who showcases confidence and self-belief.

Okay, but how do you upgrade your identity starting right now if you have been playing victim or suffering with unworthiness, laziness, or lack of self-worth for all these years? Let's get specific here with tangi-ble nuggets for you to apply immediately. Step one: grab your journal. At the top of the page, write how the highest most complete and abun-dant version of yourself would show up in the world. Now let's start making a list of the characteristics of that future version of you. What time would you wake up, go to sleep, what would you eat, what would you wear, what would be the quality of your thoughts? Get specific here so you can create a visual of an avatar of yourself that makes you feel good and worthy of all the bliss and abundance life has to offer. Can you picture this version of yourself? Would you possibly lose some weight? Would you work out? If so, what type of exercise? Would this version of you spend more time with your family? Would you love your career? Would you love yourself more, most importantly? Now we're getting somewhere. There is such power in writing and being able to create a detailed specific future version of yourself that you would bet on to win in life.

Your current reality is not a life sentence. It's just temporary. Just read-ing this book is a step in the right direction, so I want to acknowledge you for that. Now, can you see that list you created for how the highest version of you would show up? I want you to begin to strive to become more and more like that person you so creatively detailed starting right now. With every decision you make from here on out, model that future version of yourself. Begin to show up in the world as that version of you would. Watch people begin to notice a major shift in your very resonance. You will become magnetic, oozing with charisma and pro-jecting an aura that people will immediately acknowledge. And more importantly, you will be getting much closer to a whole new you that the world has not experienced yet. A person of interest, impact, prosperity, and a whole lot more fun.

This chapter alone has shown you the importance of upgrading your identity and exactly how to begin. My suggestion, don't ever stop adding to that list of ever growing improving characteristics of how the highest version of you would show up. Most importantly, don't ever stop striving to become that person. Fall in love with the process and embrace this journey. This will make you a better person, parent, child, friend, business partner, and everything in between. This will make you an upgraded human being. From this new upgraded identity you can begin to show up in congruence with the person you desire to be and you can begin to make major moves. Make waves, put a dent in the universe and really shake things up. Own this new identity and become it. Now from this upgraded identity we can resume this book with a heightened ability to consume the information and be more likely to apply it with great success.

Ask Yourself: What are five habits or skills you can begin to incorporate into your life right now to raise the standard of your identity?

15

The Truth about Entrepreneurship

If opportunity doesn't knock, build a door.

— *Milton Berle*

WHAT'S BETTER THAN being your own boss, having no ceiling on what you can create, the money that you can earn, or the impact you want to make on the world? Well, everything comes with a price. Entrepreneurship is a much different arena than any safe or stable job. There is no guarantee that you will earn a certain amount of income, but you can count on the highest of highs and the lowest of lows. I'm smiling while I write this chapter because there's literally nothing more fun than the journey, the problem solving, and figuring it all out. Well, the honest truth is that we will never fully figure it all out. That's the true spirit of the entrepreneur. It's embracing the uncertainty and leaning into the possibility of chaos.

I feel it's part of my responsibility to let you know what it actually takes to be successful in this world of entrepreneurship. I currently speak all over the world, have one of the biggest podcasts on the planet, have a massive rapidly growing community, a lucrative book deal, and have big partnerships and sponsorships with brands all over the world. I'm very self-aware, and I realize that this all looks sexy, fun, and exciting. Let me confirm, it is all those things. But what did it take to get to this level? What sacrifices were made? What relationships were severed, and how much time and energy were allocated to this? The answer is a ton. Every ounce of me was invested into CLS, mentally, emotionally, spiritually, and financially. Would I trade it back? Not even for a billion. Why? Because I'm changing lives, and having the most fun of my life, leaning into my purpose and being aligned with my life mission and assignment.

The first few months in the pandemic, I worked 20-hour days and loved every second of it. If you don't love this stuff, if you're not clear on your why and you don't negotiate the price in advance, you are doomed. Entrepreneurship is not for the faint of heart. It will beat you to your knees, make a grown man cry, and have you second-guessing yourself all night long. Yet it's been the ride of a lifetime. Once you get over that hump, and you truly become available and begin to figure

66

things out, it gets smoother and a bit less rocky. I want to be clear for the reader that sees the meteoric rise of CLS and my reinvention and thinks it's easy. It is absolutely not easy! However, if you're all in, you can take a few shots to the gut, and you're willing to stay in the fight, you will create a life to die for—abundance, wealth, impact and a full heart. I personally think it's riskier to play it safe and live with the what-if scenario. What if you went for it? What if you took a shot? What if it all worked out? When I was about to apply my three Rs and step into this arena, the scariest of all the possible scenarios was to not take my shot. My message is too important, and so is yours.

I can't say that entrepreneurship is for everyone, and I want to be clear as a person of influence to reveal what it actually takes to succeed and what the stakes are. Now, at 37-years young and having experience, success, and my share of setbacks on Wall Street and in entrepreneurship, there is nothing like the thrill of a limitless canvas to operate from. You will feel lonely and if you're in a relationship or dating during those beginning stages, your partner must absolutely be on board and supportive. If your partner isn't in alignment with the lifestyle and stress that comes with this journey, it's gonna be an uphill battle for sure. On the other hand, having a ride-or-die supportive muse or partner can enhance and elevate your game and spirit to a whole other level. I am very blessed to have that with Olesya. When I began the journey, I was single and spent a lot of time building and grinding. But timing is everything, and as I began to cultivate a ton of momentum I became available for the right partner.

Most people from your past are not going to get it, or worse, they may be critical of your path. This may be out of love, possibly from your parents or close friends, or there may be jealousy from people who look at you going for it and feel that jealousy because they didn't have the courage themselves to take their shot. Either way, my suggestion here is to stay the course, and be selective of anyone's opinions on your journey. Mostly everyone from my past life had no idea what I was doing when I began to post inspirational content and show up on social media. Most of them clap for me now and are fans, but I am sure there are still some people who resent that I totally reinvented myself to pursue my passions while others tend to live a comfortable life full of complacency and regret. It is what it is, and I genuinely wish everyone the best on their journeys and hope they live with purpose.

Enough about the risks and potential loneliness that comes with the journey. Let's talk about all the rewards, prosperity, and fulfillment that this life provides. I imagine everyone unapologetically wants to manufacture wealth, hopefully for the right reasons, so you can do great things with the money. Well, entrepreneurs are able to make the most money because there are no limits or ceilings as you head down your path of creation, collaboration, and investing in the things that align with you. The relationships I've made on this journey have been some of the most rewarding aspects on the ride, as I continue to meet, collaborate, and become friends with all the juggernauts in the space, many of whom I looked up to for years who have now become my dearest friends.

As you embark on this journey you will begin to grow rapidly as a human and you evolve. As a result, many of the associations from your last season of life begin to fade away due to being out of alignment. You make new friends with similar individuals who are more aligned with the person you are becoming. It's crazy to think that sharpening the axe, as I like to say, has become my life. In fact, talking about growth, business, and self-improvement are mostly my dinner conversations as well. Sometimes my fiancée will have to say, "Craig, let's turn our brains off for a moment" and she likes to turn on something that, respectfully, doesn't require a whole lot of thought, such as the TV show *The Office*. I should probably do a bit better job and be able to disconnect here and there, but honestly I'm obsessed with growth. I love to talk about growth in all capacities, and the subject never gets boring to me. The best part about your evolution as a human is you attract into your life the people and things that you desire at this current version of yourself.

Entrepreneurship has given me a life that makes me happier than ever before. I feel more fulfilled, I have more opportunities and fun, and I also have beautiful challenges and obstacles that really come down to problem solving. The ability to travel and work from anywhere on my laptop, to create space for creative thinking, to be able to pursue my own individual goals and dreams, and to share my message with the world has been the ride of my life, and we're just getting warmed up. If you choose to get on this road, you can make a real difference in the world and do a whole lot of good things for the world, for yourself, and for your family. If you're entrepreneurial and curious, take the shot. After all, we only get one shot at this beautiful blessing that is life.

Ask Yourself: What's something worth trying that would make you very fulfilled and excited if you could make it your career?

16

The Greatest Showman

Comfort is the enemy of progress.

– P.T. Barnum

I'M A MOVIE guy. In fact, movies are my jam. I love the experience of going to the theater, lights off, totally engaged in an adventure, and extracting a message from the film to apply to life. I typically will only create time for movies that land an impactful lesson or something that makes me better these days. One of my favorite movies of all time, one that I could throw on in the background while I'm working literally at any time, is *The Greatest Showman*. The movie stars Hugh Jackman portraying the real life P.T. Barnum. Barnum was a visionary and an entrepreneur who is most well known for founding the Barnum & Bailey circus. He reinvented himself late in life and made a full pivot to going all in on his vision—one that he was both passionate about and that would bring joy to the world. I mean, who doesn't love the circus? I remember seeing this movie and being totally captivated and blown away by all the nuggets I received. I actually took notes throughout the film. Barnum talks about comfort being the enemy of progress. Boy, did this one hit me in the teeth at a time when I was admittedly way too comfortable and just coasting at a job and relationship that didn't feel in alignment with my core. I was comfortable, I suppose, but the truth is I was scared to ask myself the tough question "Am I really happy?"

I think at some point we all get trapped into our comfort zone. This is dangerous. Sometimes we need a reminder that this time here on earth is a short trip. It could be over in the blink of an eye, and even if we live to 100 years old, we have to make every second count. Sometimes we need a good reminder of this to make sure we stay growth hungry and impact driven. My intention is that The Reinvention Formula will help you with this. Sometimes along our journeys we get an unexpected injection of inspiration, as I did from this film. There's a scene in which Barnum tells Zac Efron's character that if he joins him on this journey that he will be indeed risking everything, but he may just find himself free. For readers who feel like they're currently in a box, or a matrix, or just coasting, this is for you. The biggest risk of all is to not take any. You want to get to the end of your life a little beat up, weathered, exhausted, and happy with your efforts. You gotta take chances in life. Barnum was at first ridiculed and scoffed at for his idea of the circus. We all get laughed at or criticized at some point especially on these type of journeys, but don't worry. These same people will applaud you sooner than later and want a piece of you.

Barnum mentions how a person's station is limited only by their imagination. My goodness, does this one hit home. We are in fact limitless abundant beings all a part of the infinite. Here's a thought. We don't create abundance. We actually create limitations to interfere with our natural birthright of being abundant. It's our imagination that either fills us up with possibilities or limitations. What will you choose to see? What could go right? Or what could go wrong? An ocean of opportunity or a prison of realistic expectations? The choice is yours. The amount of nuggets of inspiration that this film and story include are unbelievable and definitely worth a watch or a rewatch. Also, whenever you watch something or hear something that really grabs you, I highly recommend writing it down in either a journal or your phone. There is a message in everything if you're available for it.

Last, to tie together the entrepreneurial journey and *The Greatest Showman*, there are a couple moments in which Barnum loses everything with regard to his business and struggles with finances. He mentions that you don't need everyone to love you. Just a few good people. This one is big. In life, you only need a handful of really loyal and supportive people in your circle especially during tough times. Let those people be your rock or your foundation of a support system. Can you have more? Absolutely, but at your core, just a couple of rock-solid humans in your corner can make all the difference when you need a shoulder to lean on, a mind to bounce ideas off, or a helping hand to lift you up. If you're all alone and you're reading this, I want you to know you are here for a reason; you can persevere and you are stronger than you realize. Shift your perspective to what can go right and take very small positive productive steps day by day and keep going. Don't ever give up.

Ask Yourself: Where can you double down on your imagination right now to expand what's possible for you?

17

The Price of Regret

We must all suffer from one of two pains: the pain of discipline or the pain of regret. The difference is discipline weighs ounces while regret weighs tons.

— Jim Rohn

THE SCARIEST THING in life I want you to fear is not what you may think. I want you to think of the cost of inaction. No action means you don't get any closer to your desires. I want you to consider fearing that whenever your time is up for this human experience, that you didn't leave a legacy, make an impact, or chase your dreams. For the reader who currently feels stuck, or is at a dead-end job, or just knows that deep down they are underachieving, know this: there is more for you out there, but you have to step up to the plate and be prepared to take some swings. Death isn't sad. The saddest thing is that most people don't live at all. Read that again. If you gravitate toward me and CLS, then you must be about growth and self-improvement.

I lived for years in a negative and unhappy state, and I began to question if there was more to life than what I was currently settling for. The key word there is *settling*. That's what I was doing in many areas of my life until I dug deep and asked myself the tough questions about whether I was really happy or making a contribution to the world. My life's work—but more specifically the last two years—has resulted in this book and formula, so that all of you don't have to settle or underachieve. Be conscious about your choices. Listen to your own intuition. Remember that the journey is what brings us happiness, not the destination. It's about getting rid of all the nonsense in your head. It's about this moment right now. Aim higher, set bigger goals, take your shots. Let's stop acting like we get a sequel to this movie.

The price of discipline is challenging and can be taxing at times. Trust me, the price of regret and wondering "what if" will eat you alive. Most of the people I know do not love what they do for a career. When I ask them why they do it, the answer is typically something along the lines of, "It's what I know," or "It pays the bills," or "I don't know what else to do." That's unacceptable to me. Why would you waste one more second existing instead of living? I see this same issue often in relationships that probably should have ended but the people in them are either comfortable or scared to be alone. What they don't seem to realize is that the moment they decide that they deserve to be happy and end a relationship that isn't healthy or honest, that they could then create space for the right relationship, partner, or person to enter their lives and provide them what they need to be happy. Don't ever settle in life, and absolutely consider the price of regret when navigating life.

When I created space to be available for CLS to be born at the beginning of the pandemic, I considered for a moment not taking my shot and going back to my miserable unfulfilling job after the lockdown was over. Then I did the eulogy exercise and I became crystal clear.

The eulogy exercise is very powerful to perform and to include in your arsenal. It goes like this: If you were to die in two weeks, who would attend your funeral? Literally visualize who would be there and more importantly, what they would say. If someone were to give your eulogy, what would they say about you? Did you make a real impact, leave a mark, have significant relationships, did you leave any sort of legacy behind? It's time to get really honest with yourself. That's the point.

For me personally, when I performed this fantastic exercise, I became brutally honest with myself and it became very obvious that although I had an amazing family and some solid relationships, that was about it. My career didn't make any sort of real contribution, I didn't change many lives, I had not created real wealth to leave behind, and I imagined I was just a spoke on the wheel of life to this point. The bottom line was that I had not fulfilled my assignment and purpose and that was not something I could live with any longer.

We all have a calling, a purpose, an assignment and it's not our *opinion* to live that out; it's our *responsibility*. This made it so real for me that I began to utilize my NLP (neuro-linguistic programming) and strategically change what I associate pain and pleasure with. This strategy is available for everyone (more to come on that shortly). I had been so unhappy, miserable, and unfulfilled that I began to associate going back to my j-o-b after the lockdown with death. This is very powerful.

Essentially the idea of choosing to go back and coast and live another moment unhappily was no longer an option. By thinking of that concept as dying a slow death, the decision I made to take my shot with CLS was a no-brainer. This is why I love when people ask me if I was scared to leave a stable and comfortable job to step into a new arena with zero experience, which also required me to completely step into uncomfortable situations such as showing up on social media and eventually on stages. Side note: Did you know that public speaking is the number one fear in America? I recently found that out and thought it was interesting.

In any event, the idea of going back to my job was the same as dying, and the eulogy exercise showed me a forward hypothetical visualization of what my legacy would be until this point, and I was not going to be a forgotten underachiever with my time here. We're blessed with this beautiful short human experience essentially on borrowed time and we have to make every second count, whatever that looks like for you. For me, I needed to burn the ships, leave the negative environment I was in, and create space for positive creative divine downloads and opportunities. So yes, let's be 100% transparent here: is taking a big swing scary? It can be, but not taking the swing, choosing to stay unhappy and unfulfilled should be the scariest thing you could ever do, and with that paradigm shift it makes the decision to take uncomfortable action and take your shot much easier and exciting. Choose your hard.

Ask Yourself: What's something exciting that you want to experience, but you have been putting off until this point?

18

Burn the Ships

Burn the boats as you enter the island and you will take the island.
— Alexander the Great

In 334 BC, ALEXANDER led a fleet of Greek and Macedonian ships across the Dardanelles Straits and into Asia Minor. When he reached the shore, Alexander ordered his men to burn the ships. He told his men, "We will either return home in Persian ships or we will die here."[1]

I feel it's my responsibility to throw a disclaimer in this chapter because I am empathetic to those who have certain responsibilities, and, for them, going all in without being able to make ends meet in the beginning should be taken on a case-by-case basis. For me personally and for many of the successful juggernauts I have become close friends with, we all agree that to energetically get behind an idea and bring it to life you have to be all in. In other words, if you're still holding on to something that's toxic and negative, you're subconsciously allocating energy to that, and as a result you're holding yourself back from putting all your positive and creative energy into the passion project. This could be a new career, passion project, or a new relationship. It applies to all. There will always be someone who is all in trying to do what you want to do, and if you're not all in, you can't possibly get to the level of success that you desire. Even if you wanted to, you can't because there is someone else who is doing everything necessary to get to that next level.

A few athletes come to mind when I think of being all in. For example, Derek Jeter from the New York Yankees didn't marry until after his professional baseball career was over because, he said, the energy and time that his partner deserved would always be lacking due to the fact that he was 100% allocating his energy to his career. What was the result of his career, you may be wondering? It was a staggering five World Series championships, 3,465 hits, numerous accolades, and a first ballot hall of famer. When that season of life ended, he then was available for a relationship and got married and started a family. The point is, he acknowledged what it takes to be one of the very best and certain sacrifices have to be made. Everything is a season, so after his season, he was able to be all in on his family. But what a legacy that legend has created.

A couple of other athletes that I should mention are the late iconic Kobe Bryant and the living legend Tom Brady, who at the time of this writing is still going. Kobe was notorious for being the hardest worker and getting to practice earlier than his teammates, staying after and working on his game. After his basketball career was over—which he was all in on, resulting in five NBA championships and an abundance of other awards—he then reinvented himself and was having a ton of success as a dad, husband, and numerous other projects such as creating a production company. He also developed a short film called *Dear Basketball*, which won an Academy Award. Let that one really marinate. Kobe had one of the most successful NBA careers ever which he was all in on; then, when that season ended, he won an Oscar by going all in on a new career. If you're not all in on your craft, your projects, your careers, or your relationships they will most likely suffer.

To be clear, you can still achieve success to a degree while not burning the ships. For example, could you be stuck at a job you don't like, but you need to pay bills, so you work on your side hustle at nights, weekends, and early mornings? Yes, you could. But let's be very specific here. If you're absolutely committed to working around that job and doing everything you can to get the side project up and running so that it eventually becomes your main thing, it could work. The issue is that a lot of people in similar positions, after a long day at the taxing job, instead of going to the library or reading about the industry they want to enter or anything else necessary to make progress say, "I'll get after it tomorrow" and they turn on Netflix or go to sleep or do basically anything else other than working on what is going to set up their future.

You can't be *interested* in something and achieve success. You have to be *committed* to doing whatever it takes with what you have with where you're at, or you have to burn the ships and remove the possibility of retreat the way I did when I said going back to Wall Street was not an option. I was going to make CLS work, and I would do whatever it took to get it off the ground, even if I had to move in with my parents to make ends meet. Clearly, that wasn't even going to be an option either, because I was all in. I believe, when you energetically go all in on something with that maniacal drive and passion, you will become creative and resourceful enough to figure it out, or the chessboard of life will move pieces around to help you along the way.

Ask Yourself: Where do you need to allocate more focus and energy in your life?

Note

1. https//mannerofspeaking.org/2015/01/03/burning-the-ships-and-sailing-away

19

The Power of Neuro-Linguistic Programming (NLP)

The future hasn't been written yet.

– Dr. Emmett Brown, *Back to the Future*

I WASN'T SOMEONE who grew up with a ton of confidence, and I wasn't exposed to personal development and self-improvement until after college—at least not in a strategic and organized capacity. As I mentioned earlier, one of the greatest and most important moments of my life was that when I got to Wall Street and felt like a fish out of water, I also stumbled upon neuro-linguistic programming (NLP). Now I wonder whether I found NLP or whether NLP found me. The jury is still out, just as it is with my introduction to the sport of running.

Everything is divine, and I became blown away and fascinated with the concepts of reprogramming your brain. I was obsessed with diving deeper into being able to alter my beliefs, changing what I associate pain and pleasure with, and cultivating confidence on command. This was my first taste of becoming mentally fit and strategic in the way I went about my life.

It's funny to me that you could ask 100 people who are familiar with the studies of NLP what it is, and you'll most likely get 100 different answers. The simplest way for me to explain it is as follows. It's an attitude and methodology that allows people to communicate more effectively. Essentially our understanding of the world is based on how we represent it, also known as our map. Our understanding is not based on the actual world itself. Rather, it's sort of like having a unique and personal perspective on how we view life and its experiences. To understand this world, we subconsciously create a map in our brains. This is why two people can look at the exact same situation and see two totally different perspectives. One may see limitations and a dead end, while the other may see opportunities and possibilities.

You're going to want to highlight this chapter and reread it numerous times so let's really focus here. This technology, if you will, changed the course of my life. It provided me with choices and organized strategies to apply to live a much more fulfilling and enriching life. Whatever you think is going on is just your map, and it doesn't necessarily match the map of the people around you. In order to become very successful and effective with this technology you need to be able to expand your map and cultivate different perspectives. Let's dive deeper.

We have cultivated subconscious processes and patterns that have turned into the recipes we follow to produce certain thoughts, feelings, and behaviors. However, by becoming aware of these patterns, we now have the option or choice to purposefully improve them or even change them entirely. I remember when I first started doing my homework on this, I sought out a mentor who could help me understand it better and begin to apply it.

During this season of life, I had been networking and often going to business dinners and meetings at which, literally every time, there was seafood or sushi served. Until this point of my life, I had developed a strong belief that I didn't like seafood, especially the smell in addition to the taste. With my new understanding of NLP and the ability to change or improve my map, I began to practice associating pleasure with seafood, especially sushi, so that I could participate in the meals at the business meetings. I realized that I wasn't born with the belief of disliking seafood. I must have picked it up along my journey. What if I changed that belief and reprogrammed my brain? This worked in a big way and— just like that, in an instant—I began to embrace the smell of seafood and to this day, a spicy tuna roll with spicy mayo is one of my favorite meals.

Imagine if you could apply this strategy to other areas of your life. How powerful is that? What if you could suddenly stop being afraid of heights? What if you could transform insecurities with an unwavering self-belief and confidence? Well, you can. NLP has helped me deliberately reshape my mindset and eliminate the stuff that was causing interference and replace it with empowering and enriching thoughts and beliefs. This is a game changer.

For readers eager to expand their outlook of the world, I want to hammer this point home. You can choose to refuse the limiting beliefs that you have today and begin to question them and replace them. As a result, you can expand your entire perspective on what's possible for you in this world. Will you choose to be a victim, or a victor? Will you select limitations or replace them with possibilities? You have a choice. Just becoming aware that we have a choice is the first big breakthrough to applying this technology with great success.

NLP has helped me in many ways, especially in building rapport and being a ninja when it comes to sales and relationships. Feelings are contagious, so if you want someone to feel elevated and good, you have to begin by going into that state yourself first. Like attracts like. People want to be around people who are high vibe, positive energy, and confident. It's contagious. Here's where it gets really fun. You can intentionally create any state you want. A tool from NLP that I love is called modeling. Let's explore this with an exercise.

Grab the journal and begin to write down the names of a bunch of people who you hold in very high regard, or even role models of yours. Make a list of about 10 on the left side of the page. On the right side of the page write down three adjectives that you admire about each role model. Now you have a list of people and attributes that you can tap into on command to enhance your state. When you're in an elevated state, you see solutions and opportunities. On the flip side, when you're in a lowered state you see problems and pessimism. I personally love modeling, and I can't recommend enough adding this tool to your toolbox moving forward. When I first got to Wall Street, totally lacking confidence and experience, I dove deep into this technique. I began to model one of my favorite movie characters, the iconic and dynamic 007 James Bond. I associated Bond with confidence, swag, charisma, and an unwavering self-belief. I began to model these attributes from the way I walked including my body language and my ability to not let rejection bother me. Now this totally elevated my performance in life, from being confident on the phone to approaching girls at bars. I began to not think about the possibility of being rejected and instead focused on being so confident that if someone wasn't interested in me, it was their loss. Being in an elevated state is so contagious and magnetic that it helps you play bigger, and it draws other people to you. I want to say this: This doesn't mean that you are pretending to be someone else. You are still you. However, if someone out there is performing in a certain way that you'd like to model or they possess characteristics that you would like to learn and develop, begin by modeling them and watch yourself grow into the person that possesses these skills. You can feel as good as you want by going into the correct state and you can literally make every single thing you do magical.

Choose a different thought. The right thought can affect your entire physiology, instantly showcasing just how powerful the mind truly is. This is why I often say that mindset is the key to life. Additionally, the next time you're feeling off or perhaps in a lowered frequency, start by wearing a big fat juicy smile. This releases happy chemicals to the rest of your body. This was discussed by my good friend Chris Voss,[1] expert former FBI negotiator and bestselling author who was a guest on the *CLS Experience* podcast. There is scientific evidence of the positive impact of a smile. Start by smiling when you enter any room moving forward and watch how you give off an aura that's confident and magnetic.

If you go into the right state or elevate your frequency using these priceless tools, you can do just about anything. Remember humans influence each other every time we communicate. Stay elevated. The best communicators in the world whom I've collaborated with know how to build great rapport with people. I take such pride in my preparation when doing homework on my guests for *The CLS Experience*. When I hit my guest with a juicy nugget about them that is not so available to most, they immediately become disarmed and impressed with the effort I put in. This makes for an amazing experience and conversation, and it immediately builds the connection between us. I remember doing this with Alicia Silverstone[2] during our episode, which totally caught her off guard and helped the interview really become intimate and compelling. The ability to build rapport and form a connection is the key to relationship building and is especially important for becoming effective at sales. Building rapport means you are tuning in.

One of the methodologies that I use with my community, clients, and audience is to help them enrich their model of the world. In NLP this is called a meta model. Being able to help someone think and play bigger is very important because it helps people find solutions and create a new perspective that displays possibilities rather than limits and constraints. I often ask questions like "What's stopping you?" or "What would happen if you could?" This helps people begin to change their way of thinking and become available for more abundance. They are able to lose some of the subconscious scarcity they have been holding on to. Asking the right questions can be so powerful in helping either yourself or others see things from a different perspective. For the person who lacks confidence or is having trouble putting themselves out there, I want to ask you this: What would happen if you weren't shy? How would your life be different if you weren't afraid to show up? This helps them consider that there is an alternative story that can be written. This is so powerful that I have chills just explaining these concepts and how they helped me cultivate confidence and replace the stories in my mind with much more empowering ones that have helped me show up more purposefully and efficiently. Bottom line: do not accept limitations! If you go into the right frequency or state, the answers about how to do things will come to you.

Here's the kicker: Just reading this and understanding this knowledge isn't going to elevate your performance. This is where you have to be very proactive with this information. It's not enough that you overcome your problems. You have to replace them with new behaviors and new thoughts that take you in a new direction. We want the lessons we learned out in front of us and the negative feelings behind us. Remember this, some things are actually worth forgetting to create a brand-new story to operate from, while some things are worth remembering. Use the tools such as modeling and anchoring, in which you can replicate a past experience when you were on fire or in a very high state and frequency, channel that to your current situation. Then, you have that at your fingertips to tap into whenever you see fit. Keep practicing going into a state of bliss, and begin to master how good you can feel for absolutely no reason at all.

These tools were the beginning of me recreating myself and molding myself like clay. Imagine yourself like a computer and you have several programs running that either enhance or decrease your performance. Essentially you can uninstall programs that slow down your software and download new ones that upgrade your skill sets. This always reminded me of the movie *The Matrix*. We begin with our thoughts, then thoughts become actions, then actions become our habits, and our habits become who we are. The best part of this work—and personal development in general—is that we are never done learning. It's so cool to me that every day we can learn new information that can help us optimize our performance in life. If we're doing something that isn't working, we can try something new. We can forget bad memories and essentially delete them from our hard drives. So to conclude this chapter, we're going to commit right now to eliminate negative thoughts and feelings that used to interfere with our lives negatively, and choose new thoughts. Thoughts that enrich our maps and cultivate new, exciting positive perspective. Now, let the fun begin.

Ask Yourself: Who is someone you hold in high regard and what impressive characteristics do they possess?

Notes

1. https://podcasts.apple.com/us/podcast/tactical-empathy-with-chris-voss/id1533716044?i=1000549598472
2. https://podcasts.apple.com/us/podcast/the-icon-with-alicia-silverstone/id1533716044?i=1000531529557

20

Setting Boundaries

"No" is a complete sentence.

– Anne Lamott

TRIGGER ALERT—THIS CHAPTER is going to make you feel some type of way. I recently started to associate pleasure with the word *no*. I'm a recovering people pleaser, and it used to not only burn me out but also keep me in this bubble of inauthenticity. Every time you say yes to something that doesn't feel good, you add a bit more inauthenticity to your identity, and worse, you potentially deplete yourself of the great vibes and energy you were operating with.

Have you ever had your mom or someone that brings a ton of energy— possibly negative energy—come over, and within five minutes you're ready for a nap? I say mom, because we all have someone, possibly a family member who is a handful, and you often find yourself exiting your interaction with them in a lowered emotional state. Yet there is that college friend or old roommate who you haven't seen in two years, and you go meet up with them, and all of a sudden you're out until three in the morning. You have no idea where time went and you could spend all day with them and feel energized and on fire. This is very real and here's why. As discussed earlier in this book, everyone is a vibe. Everyone has a frequency. We have the choice of which Wi-Fi we want to tune in to. Now I want you to give yourself some grace if you've been around someone before and left the experience feeling off or negged out or just not yourself. I wrestled with this for a bit before I totally understood it. I would be hard on myself and think how does that person have the power to lower my state? Why would I be available to let that happen? Here's the truth. We are human and energy is powerful. After all, we've already acknowledged that this is a vibrational universe. To manifest abundance we have to be a vibrational match for it and allow it to come in. Well, there are certain people out there that have their own strong and powerful vibe, and as we learned in the NLP chapter, if your map is out of alignment with their map, you may often disagree with them or even butt heads at times, because of the totally different ways you both view the world or your maps of it.

In order to stay in that elevated vibrational state, in which you are attracting abundance and great experiences, you have to be so intentional with who and what you allow into your bubble of serenity. My view is this. If it's not a "Hell, yes," then it's a "Hell, no." You have to fill your cup first and take time to replenish your energy and do a good job of keeping it high and optimal. This may mean that you begin to distance yourself from previous relationships that diminish your light. In return, you'll stay in that higher frequency and become available for new relationships that match your frequency and are in alignment with who you are and who you are becoming.

On an airplane before each flight the flight attendants do a little presentation. They show how to use the oxygen masks and they demonstrate putting one on yourself first, then the child or partner you are with. Now why is that? At the end of the day if you're not in good shape, you're no good to help anyone. You have to selfishly prioritize your own well-being, specifically your emotional and mental state. We need you on fire and available and energetic so that you can operate at an elite level and make an impact.

Now, I can hear the questions coming in right now: "But how do I spend less time with my family or my friends?" Look, no one said this was going to be easy and I want to be crystal clear, I don't want anyone to cut out their family entirely. However, maybe you don't take that midday call from that friend or family member who wants to gossip and talk about nothing productive, and you postpone that conversation to later at night or let them know the next time you speak that you are setting boundaries moving forward. You are absolutely available to them to support them or catch up, but you are no longer interested in meaningless dialogue and definitely not here to gossip. Gossip and jealousy are very strong negative emotions that the universe doesn't like—trust me—and are a waste of everyone's time. In this way, the family member or friend that you are now setting boundaries with is not being cut off. You have supplied them with a choice. They can either grow and evolve with you or not, and based on how they respond, you can act accordingly. Look, this is one of the toughest chapters in the book, but it is also one of the most rewarding once you begin to distance yourself from negative energy that used to deplete you. This changes the whole game.

Here's the beauty of it. As you begin to set boundaries and practice saying the word *no*, you become less available for those vibes that used to diminish your productivity, and you become wide open and available for the people or things that nourish you. A question I always like to ask myself and my clients is this: Does it nourish you? If the answer is yes, get after it. If the answer is no, reconsider it.

Look, we all have that group of friends from high school or college or even camp with whom you all share great memories and inside jokes. Perhaps they haven't changed much over the years, and you continue to evolve and you don't want to cut them out entirely. Here's my suggestion. Have an understanding with yourself that when you go meet them for dinner, the conversations will most likely be about the glory days and Netflix or whatever they are into. Just know that's okay for that time you allocated to them. There will most likely not be dialogue about sharpening the axe or growth and expansion. I would suggest you be intentional with that time and limit those interactions, but also give yourself grace that when you get together with that group that's what it is and embrace it. But if you have a group or person that literally crushes your vibe, then I would suggest saying no to it. If it's your family, then you have to be transparent about how you would like to feel leaving an interaction with them, and ask them for their support. If you continue to spend time with them and find yourself depleted, then you have to make some tough decisions.

This goes for events, places, and experiences as well. If you find that when you drink alcohol, you find yourself lowering your productivity the next day or you don't feel great and you lose momentum, then perhaps it's time to reconsider some of your choices in all areas of life. You have to protect your energy as if your life depended on it. The world needs you at your highest frequency, and making the choice to entertain people or things that lower your state make you less likely to change the world or operate in an ineffective manner.

Be unapologetic about protecting your energy. Act as if you only get one shot at this beautiful ride that is life. Find new tribes—join a networking group or community that is full of people on your wavelength. This is exactly why I created the CLS Membership[1]—to create a space where like-minded growth-oriented people can connect and support each other. No one should be perceived as having a hall pass to be in your life forever. The sooner you realize that, the easier this becomes. Most people are in your life for a season and a reason. They bring you joy and purpose for that particular season and you both move on. Hopefully your family and life partner are this exception. Nurture the relationships of course. Do not feel guilty for outgrowing people, because at the end of the day, we are meant to grow, expand, and spread our wings and evolve. Everyone else has an opportunity to grow with you. Don't feel bad for making decisions that hurt other people; you're not responsible for their happiness, only your own.

Ask Yourself: Where in your life can you create addition by subtraction?

Note

1. https://www.cultivatelastingsymphony.com/membership

21

Owning Your Story

You either walk inside your story and own it or you stand outside your story and hustle for your worthiness.

— Brené Brown

SPOILER ALERT—WE ALL have a past. There's a lot of good in there and a lot of not so good. People become addicted to suffering by holding on to the past and replaying certain stories in their mind. The body has the stress hormone cortisol. When stressors are always present and you constantly feel under attack, that fight-or-flight reaction stays turned on causing an excessive amount of stress and a feeling of addiction toward staying in this lowered state or vibration. The constant exposure of cortisol and other stress hormones that follow can disrupt almost all your body's functions, putting you at an increased risk of many health problems. As you can already tell, this creates a snowball effect of feeling badly. Some of the effects from a large amount of stress or cortisol built up can be anxiety, depression, headaches, sleep issues, and a whole lot more. Why are we talking about this?

Here's the breakthrough. It's so important that we learn healthy ways to cope or respond to life stressors and experiences. You may know people who seem relaxed about almost everything and others who react strongly to the slightest stress. Most people react to life stressors somewhere between those extremes.

Look, stressful events are facts of life. They are inevitable. You can take steps to manage the impact these events have on you. You can learn to identify what causes you stress and how to take care of yourself physically and emotionally in the face of stressful situations. I wanted to take a moment and identify that cortisol actually creates more stress and more suffering, so what we have to do is stop this in its tracks and begin a new pattern of feeling good. We can create and produce more of the positive hormones such as dopamine, serotonin, and endorphins. These are well known for being the feel-good and happy hormones that elevate our state and keep us in an enhanced frequency—sort of like a natural high-on-life feeling of bliss. I want to dive in on choosing a new story from your past so that you can begin to forgive yourself for what has happened, and you can start with a clear, fresh, positive outlook and to begin to climb out of the negative thoughts and beliefs of what's behind you.

Forgive yourself. If you're not where you want to be or had hoped that you would be at this point in your life, forgive yourself and own every part of it—all the crap that's happened in your past, all of it. The bad decisions, the bankruptcy, the divorce, the investments, the unfulfilling career path, the toxic relationships, all of it. All of this happened *for* you, not *to* you and you are now qualified to move forward and inspire others with what you've been through and overcame. Let that digest and marinate for a moment. My friend Major League Baseball legend Darryl Strawberry,[1] who was a guest on the *CLS Experience* podcast, illustrates his transformation and all the dark seasons of his life, and I mean the *darkest* of times. He talks about how his perspective changed from victim mentality to victor by altering the way he looked at his past and adopting a new outlook that he was actually being qualified to start a new mission, impacting millions of people realizing that they too can bounce back from rock bottom.

Look, we all have pasts and we all have skeletons in our closets. There are some things that we have the power to change and many things that we can't change. But the most important thing that we can change right now is how we feel about ourselves and our past. Give yourself some grace. You're reading this book right now so clearly you are on the path to reinvention and becoming the best version of you that the world has ever witnessed. I myself lived in that victim mentality for a long time years ago. I was feeling sorry for myself and frustrated with some of the choices I made, as well as feeling unworthy to create a life with a new direction and purpose. When I made the decision to give birth to the Reinvention Formula, one of the most powerful things I did was forgive myself and stand on top of my story as opposed to inside my story. Run that back and write it down.

After waking up one day in that past situation, finding myself single, unhappy with my career path, and lacking a direction or purpose, I decided—before I had any clarity on CLS or any idea about totally pivoting from my career—to create my 2020 Journal Entry with the theme of the Rise. I am a huge journaler, and every year in December

I create a very intentional journal entry that has a theme for the upcoming year that I will lean into and manifest. I reflect on the year that passed, the great and not so great, and most importantly I set my intentions for the year ahead. I highly suggest everyone begin to do this as well. I look back now at all my yearly journal entries over the last few years and the theme name for each is an exact indication of how that upcoming year will turn out. Coincidence? I think not. This is goal setting, intention allocating, and manifesting at its core.

Heading into 2020 with no concrete plans or knowledge of a lock-down or CLS, I did know one thing for sure. I was committed to forgiving myself for being in the unfulfilled and unhappy spot I was in, and I was ready to become available for a new direction and let go of the past history that kept me in a mental prison. This didn't mean that I had to approve of my past and all the choices that led me to that point, but it did mean that I had to accept them. And there is great power in acceptance, because now you can take positive inspired action to change your path acknowledging that a new path is necessary.

I get that one of the toughest things to do is to let go of your past and start fresh. However it is also one of the most important and powerful choices you can make. Life has happened *for* you, not *to* you. You have been qualified to show up and help others who may be dealing with things that you went through and overcame. You are also battle tested and seasoned and hard to kill. Not dead, not done. You are here, so be here. Take the past that you're ashamed of and feel guilt toward and begin to own it. Yes it's true you are not perfect. No one is. Do you think you're more valuable to the world operating out of a frequency of shame, guilt, and regret, or do you think you can contribute more by owning your past and allowing it to strengthen your resolve, creating a more bulletproof mindset and an unwavering ability to endure and keep moving forward?

Sometimes the key to life and business is just staying in the fight. We cannot exist in our pity party and feel paralyzed to move forward due to a negative belief system created from things that are behind us. That does no one any good. The world needs you and your gifts, and some of your gifts are actually your ability to overcome what you did. Bottom line, do not surrender all your joy for an idea or negative belief that you used to have about yourself that is no longer true. Please, run that back and read it again. Consider your options right now. As I see it, there is only one. Keep going and become a better, more experienced and resilient person because of your past. If you have gotten your heart broken before in the past, does that mean you should live as a victim and never open your heart again for the possibility of love and finding your person? Of course not.

Learn from your past, give yourself grace from some of the mistakes and choices, and stand on top of those lessons more powerful, authentic, vulnerable and stronger because of them. Own your story. It's yours, no one else's. It's your movie. Maybe you haven't loved the script or some of the plot twists, but the pen is in your hand to rewrite the next chapter. Will you choose victimhood and pity parties that result in being paralyzed with trauma from your past or take responsibility and ownership for everything that has happened for you, and become better because of your experiences? Choose your hard. Sometimes your old life has to fall apart before your new life can fall together. Don't hesitate to leave the past in the past. This is not how your story ends. It's simply where it takes a turn you didn't expect.

Ask Yourself: What part of your story do you need to own and accept in order to set it free?

Note

1. https://podcasts.apple.com/us/podcast/turn-the-season-around-with-darryl-strawberry/id1533716044?i=1000571154591

22

The Four-Minute Mile

If you don't clap when you see others win, you're missing the point.

– *Craig Siegel*

FOR YEARS, EXPERTS said it was unattainable to run a four-minute mile. It couldn't be done. They claimed the achievement was not only humanly impossible but even life-threatening. The human body simply couldn't run a four-minute mile without the person's heart exploding. This perception kept the accomplishment unachievable, and culture and society believed that it was not a thing. People surrendered to this belief, and as a result the world records hovered above that mark for a lifetime. Until . . .

Mythology illustrates that people had tried for over a thousand years to break the barrier, even tying bulls behind them to increase the incentive to do the unimaginable. Then, in the 1940s, the mile record was pushed to 4.01, where it stood for a staggering nine years, as runners struggled with the idea that, just maybe, the experts had it right. Perhaps the human body had reached its capacity. Then there was a massive breakthrough. There was a new unique mental approach. Let's dive deeper. Story time.

On May 6, 1954, Roger Bannister, a 25-year-old medical student, worked his typical morning shift at St. Mary's Hospital and took an afternoon train from Paddington Station to Oxford in preparation for a one-mile race against Oxford University. For nearly 10 years, until that day, Bannister ran mostly out of fear to escape bullies and aerial bombs he heard during the Battle of Britain in World War II. "I imagined bombs and machine guns raining on me if I didn't go my fastest," he wrote in his memoirs. Despite his enthusiasm for running, Bannister wasn't exactly a top running prospect. His commitment as a full-time medical student on regular hospital shifts left him with little time to train. His training was limited to a relatively short half-hour sessions three times a week. Additionally, his lack of coaching forced him to create his own system to prepare for races. Shortly after Bannister arrived at Iffley Road Track in Oxford, nearly 1,200 spectators gathered to witness the race under moist weather conditions. Six runners, including Bannister, prepared to run the most important race of their lives.

Like Roger, the better part of mile runners had one goal in mind aside from winning. They wanted to break the yet to be accomplished four-minute mile. Since 1886, the most talented runners and best coaches had given their all and yet failed to run a mile in under four minutes. According to Bannister, the four-minute mile had become "rather like an Everest—a barrier that seemed to defy all attempts to break it—an awesome reminder that man's striving might be in vain."

At 6.00 p.m., the race kicked off. Two runners, Brasher and Chataway, took the lead during the first three minutes of the race. On the final leg of the race with less than 275 yards to go, Bannister powered through with his signature explosive kick, took the lead and won the race in dramatic fashion. There was a spooky silence all around the stadium as the crowd held their breath to hear the announcement of the race times. Then suddenly, the race commentator announced that Roger Bannister, a medical student, had set a new World Record time of 3 minutes 59.4 seconds, becoming the first-ever person in history to break the mythical barrier of the four-minute mile. But the story isn't over yet.

Within 46 days, Bannister's rival, John Landy, ran a four-minute mile and broke the record with a time of 3 minutes 57.9 seconds. A year later, three runners ran four-minute miles in a single race. By the end of 1978, over 200 runners had broken the once impossible barrier of the four-minute mile.

"One of the best explanations for this phenomenon is the theory of self-efficacy developed by the renowned psychologist, Albert Bandura. According to Bandura, self-efficacy is defined as "beliefs in one's capabilities to organize and execute the courses of action required to produce given attainments."[1] In other words, "self-efficacy refers to an individual's belief in his or her capacity to execute behaviors necessary to produce specific performance attainments."[2] The self-efficacy theory suggests that individuals with high self-efficacy are more likely to take the most action toward their goals, persist in the face of adversity, and push the barriers of what they believe is possible. They are also more likely to tap into states of flow that improve mental and physical performance. Let's get down to the nitty gritty here.

What's most important here is that Bannister broke the psychological barrier that had held back the greatest runners for over a century. Other runners now believed that it was possible. It is no surprise then that several other runners broke the four-minute mile too. For the majority of us who will never attempt to break a running record, the four-minute mile represents the limiting beliefs of what we think is possible to achieve in our lives. We tend to limit our goals in business, relationships, finance, health, and our careers, within the arena of what society says is possible or impossible. But throughout history, there are a handful of people like Roger, who break the limits of what's possible and leave a lasting legacy and demonstrate what is attainable, which is the real kicker here. What makes them different isn't their talent, skills, or resources, but their belief system. They'd rather take the lead, step outside their comfort zones, and risk failure, rather than wait in their comfort zones for permission from others to achieve the impossible. Followers wait for leaders to show them what's possible. Leaders break the barriers of what's possible. Which one will you choose to be?

As part of his training, he relentlessly visualized the achievement in order to create a sense of certainty in his mind and body. Let's run that back for a moment. Roger relentlessly visualized the end result, creating a feeling of already having accomplished this feat that was once thought to be impossible, thereby creating a feeling within the body that it was completed, and time just hadn't caught up yet. So now Roger showcased a new possibility. Now that benchmark has become routine.

Let's unpack this. Did the runners suddenly become faster? Did the shoes provide the ultimate cheat code for running a sub-four-minute mile? Unlikely. Let's talk about what really happened here. What does this mean for us?

For me, a four-minute mile is probably not in the cards, although I wouldn't entirely rule it out, it's just not something I'm interested in. That's not the point. The point is this. It took a sense of extreme certainty for Roger Bannister to do what was considered undoable. He alone was able to create that certainty in himself without seeing any proof that it could be done. He was unplugged from the matrix, as I like to say, and where literally everyone else saw limits, constraints, and a ceiling, Roger saw possibilities and opportunities. He believed that life is meant to be abundant. He did the inner work. He combined his mental fitness with his physical fitness. Once he crashed through that barrier, the rest of the world saw that it was possible, and now it's the standard and considered the benchmark for these runners.

I'm obsessed with this story for many reasons. You may argue that this was the law of attraction or perhaps this was his RAS (reticular activating system) in full effect. The RAS is discussed in great detail in almost every self-help and personal development book so I'll keep this short and simple. The RAS helps you to start filtering those pieces that can help you with your intention, and so the subconscious mind brings that into your conscious mind, so you start to see and hear and understand the things that will help you get to what you're intending. If you want to get a new watch such as a Rolex or a brand-new Mercedes car, all of a sudden you begin to see those specific things everywhere you look, even though they have been there all along, now you're hyperfocused on seeing them. When you become absolutely certain of something, when every part of your wiring believes it because you focus on it every single day, something magical and special occurs. This isn't some woo-woo crazy controversial magic; this is science magic. The reticular activating system (RAS) helps our brains decide what information to focus on and what to delete. When you have a clearly defined purpose, a mission, and when you live every moment in a state of certainty that you'll achieve it, you influence what your RAS filters out and what lights it up. As a result, you pay special attention to things that help you achieve what you're after, things you otherwise would have never noticed.

What I love about Roger's approach was his unwavering level of certainty that this could be done. Self-belief is where everything begins, especially your reinvention. Why should you clap when you see others winning?

When I first got to Wall Street feeling like a fish out of water, I remember my first day inside the high energy and wild office. I took a moment to observe. I looked around, asked some questions, and saw many people who were doing very well for themselves in terms of financial success. At that season of my life, I was motivated by financial success. I remember having this very important realization. Where most rookies in a whole new arena may feel intimidated or a sense of imposter syndrome and unworthiness, I couldn't help but think that, if these guys were making so much money, then it was only a matter of time before I gained the experience and knowledge and, combined with my unmatched work ethic, would be able to surpass them. I was captivated and excited because these other brokers at the time were crushing it, and it showed me what was possible. On the flip side, if I entered a new arena and saw that the top producers were not making much money or having much success, it would have limited my imagination on what I could possibly accomplish. Seeing others win in life, particularly in an environment that you'd like to enter, illustrates possibilities and opportunities.

I carried this same mindset, although motivated differently these days, to my reinvention when I stepped into the personal development arena and more specifically the online world. People get scared because they think it's congested and oversaturated. Spoiler alert, it is. But with a different perspective I like to say this. There's always room for the best. Now for me, I'm motivated by impact, changing lives, and making a difference. So as I begin to step into this world, continue to become more and more mentally fit, and put in the work and ask for help, it's pretty much a guarantee that it's only a matter of time before I can contribute in a big way. After all, I'm not just interested. I'm not even just committed. I'm all in. Seeing other people achieve success is a great sign that you too can do great things. Clap when you see others win. Remember you're not competing with anyone else, only yourself and getting better each day.

Additionally it's also good positive energy to congratulate and acknowledge others that are winning. There's no jealousy here. There's more than enough abundance to go around for everyone to win. Take that into consideration anytime you feel some sort of way when you see someone from your past or anyone in your world begin to get further ahead. Adopt the mentality that if they can, so can you.

I have this same mindset in all areas of my life including running. When I see friends in the running world hit new personal records and run crazy times, I immediately think to myself, wow if they can run that, what am I capable of if I level up with my nutrition and education on the sport? Clap when you see others win, they are showing you what's possible out there, and now all you have to do is gain the resources and support system to go out and leave your mark on the world.

Ask Yourself: What limitations can you replace with possibilities?

Notes

1. https://www.mayooshin.com/four-minute-mile
2. https://beconomics.commons.gc.cuny.edu/self-efficacy

23

Relationship Capital

Success leaves clues, proximity is power. Love your family, choose your peers.
— Tony Robbins

It's IRONIC THAT Craig 1.0 used to take pride in attempting to figure everything out by myself. When I gave birth to CLS, reinvented myself, and began my new life, I realized that being stubborn and attacking all the tasks and skills alone was way too time consuming and absolutely not the best use of my time and energy. I made the decision to put my ego aside and embrace the fact that I don't know what I don't know. I began to utilize my NLP tools and changed my perspective from associating pain with asking for help to associating pleasure with gaining support and the wisdom of others. I began to look at mentorship as a cheat code for success and the best way to accelerate my growth, so I can then extend my reach and make the biggest impact possible.

There's a reason why Tom Brady and Michael Jordan had coaches, right? They don't just come out of the locker room and hit the game with no guidance or game plan. A coach or mentor helps you navigate the adventure that is life. They can help you minimize some of the potential mistakes and obstacles by jumping on them from the beginning and being prepared.

Proximity also provides a way for you to enter an arena with people who are not necessarily better than you, but, rather, further along. See what they're doing right, observe how they operate, ask them questions, bounce ideas off them. Just getting in the rooms with these juggernauts is contagious. You begin to think and behave differently. You cultivate an edge by being around successful people. As Tony Robbins says, "Success leaves clues," and you begin to get exposed to what works and how the very best at their craft produce great results. Even just consuming the content of the greats is productive, if you can't get in the rooms.

I had proximity to the greats for years without even realizing it by listening to their podcasts and reading their books. It's important to stay curious, examine what works, and model the greats. If you spend some time with someone who is essentially sitting in the seat that you'd like to sit in, what do you think is going to happen? You're going to expand your map of the world and become available to other approaches and strategies. Take what you like, leave the rest, and continue to absorb attributes and skill sets of the people who are obtaining the impact and results that you desire. There is no better way to get ahead in a timely fashion than to be in proximity to those that are inside the arena.

In the world that I play in now, you'd be surprised how much people want to help you. It's a beautiful thing. As long as you're humble, hungry, and a go-getter, people will extend their hands to support and guide you. Don't be afraid to invest in mentorship such as a coach and masterminds. The right ones can elevate you in a big way. Regardless of the industry you're in or want to enter, having someone to support you with a fresh perspective is absolutely priceless. Masterminds allow you to not only gain knowledge and information, but you form a new circle of like-minded cats that are in alignment with who you are becoming. You make friends, and you build your network. We've all heard the expression it's not what you know, but, rather, who you know. I have to say there's a lot of truth in that. Your network is going to play a pivotal role in your reinvention. You want to be a phone call away from a big ask if need be.

As you continue to flourish and spread your wings, you will also want to give back and help others come up with you. I think it's important to always have a mentor and a mentee. Someone to learn from and someone to teach. When I began to cultivate this mindset of asking for support and creating great proximity it changed everything for me. One of my first mentors a decade ago, before I even identified what a mentor was, was my NLP teacher who taught me all the tools and techniques to help create a much better, more versatile, and equipped Craig. I started working with him in the beginning of my Wall Street days when I really wanted to grow as a human, cultivate confidence, and begin to understand how to think bigger and expand my map or potential. I remember I used to go see him once a week and he'd have to kick me out by the end of our one-hour session. I would always say "just one more question" and eventually he would have to say, "Craig, our time is up for today, I have to get home for dinner."

I'm laughing right now as I write about this because it's taking me back. This was way back before CLS was born, but the writing was always on the wall. When I was introduced to personal development I became obsessed with working on myself. You can't necessarily always count on other people in your life, but one thing you can count on is yourself. I found a mentor in the beginning stages of CLS, as well as someone who became one of my really good friends, David Meltzer. He's further ahead than I am, has about 17 years on me, and has a lot more life experience and wisdom. It's a beautiful thing when mentors become your closest friends.

Bottom line is as follows: Make the most important investment you will ever make in this life, and invest in yourself. Be available for mentorship, coaches, masterminds, and communities to accelerate your growth. Let's be honest about something, we don't have forever in this human experience. We have to play chess and be intentional and strategic in how we make the most of our time. What seems like a more effective approach here: trying to do everything yourself and figure it all out or surround yourself with the people who are sitting in the seat that you'd like to be in? Pretty simple to me. It's why I'm so passionate about The CLS Membership,[1] because I know the impact of community. That's why I created what I've been told by anyone that's anyone that our community is the most dynamic and supportive tribe out there. If you're looking for a place to begin, that's a great place to start. We discuss strategies, mindset, entrepreneurship, life, business, relationships, and everything in between. We also have massive guest speakers come in and my favorite part of all, a private group where everyone networks and supports each other. It's time to bet on yourself, take uncomfortable action, and be in proximity of people who are a bit further ahead, so you can double down on your own personal growth. Thank me later.

Ask Yourself: What room do you need to get in or who is a bit further ahead that you need to be around?

Note

1. https://www.cultivatelastingsymphony.com/membership

24

Divine Intervention

The best motivating factor of all, however, is divine intervention or what I like to call the magic of grace.

— Cheryl Richardson

IF YOU'RE LOOKING for a surface level chapter, this will not be the one for you. We're going deep below with this one. I have really worked on and prioritized my relationship with God over the past 10 years, but I really doubled down in 2020 when I asked him to reveal himself in the most amazing of ways at the start of the pandemic and lockdown. If you're going to believe in a higher being, something you could call supernatural, why not engage in supernatural conversations, and so I did. Since then we communicate daily and in the most fascinating ways. There is no stronger confidence than knowing that God has your back, and choosing to believe in something bigger than yourself. Now, it may be God, the universe, the quantum, Jesus, or Hanukkah Harry, but I think it's essential that you have something that works for you.

I'm not going to tell you who you should believe in, I am only going to share how this process has elevated my life in ways I could have never imagined. First and foremost, having faith relieves you of any disasters or massive setbacks, because you always have this underlying belief that it will all work out because you're not alone. For the reader who has a strong faith already, this will add to it, and for the reader who lacks or struggles with a deeper understanding and belief in faith, I challenge you to be open-minded here and lean in.

One of the most powerful cures for self-doubt, is the very thought and concept that you are not alone in this world. You have a companion who is always looking out for you and protecting and propelling you to something greater. If you cultivate faith, nothing will be impossible for you. It reminds me of the expression that everything that happens is 10% the event and 90% our attitude toward it. That means that life happens *for* us and not *to* us, and if we can choose a positive attitude about it and everything else, we cannot only get through the toughest of times, but we will never be crippled with doubt, fear, and a loss of hope, because we know we are always being protected in some capacity. Consider the alternative here for a moment. Let's say you didn't have faith. How would you be able to bounce back from tough situations and maintain a positive mindset after really challenging life setbacks?

With my faith and belief in God growing every single day, it makes obstacles so much easier to overcome. For example, when I received the tumor diagnosis in my foot, I gave myself grace and allowed the feelings in, but the next day I took an attitude that, although I may not understand right now, I know this is happening for me and God is watching over me. By choosing this attitude, it's nearly impossible to stay down in a lowered emotional state for very long because you know it's all a part of your journey and story. Had I not had faith at that difficult time, I would have easily entertained a very long and unproductive pity party, which would have done the world and me no good. Having faith also makes you available to see options and opportunities, such as me deciding to run the NYC Marathon after the surgery, inspire my father, raise money for the American Cancer Society, and inspire millions in the CLS community. Although I didn't have the physical training to safely attempt to tackle the 26.2 miles, I had something much more important. I had faith and intuition. I consider this whole life event to be divine intervention. The impact I was able to make post-surgery and post-tumor was far greater than any individual accolades or accomplishment I would have gained just for running the Chicago Marathon for my own personal desires.

I never appreciated it when someone would really preach and try to convince me of their own faith or whomever they believed in, because it felt weird to me and not organic. I think it's important for everyone to have their own interpretation and personal perspective and experience with faith, but I will say one of the most important things you'll ever do is to explore it. See what you gravitate toward and what feels good for you, and be open and available. Over the last two years I have had multiple divine intervention experiences and here's one that I will never forget.

In 2022 I was hit by a speeding car, in a hit-and-run in New York City. Manhattan has become a bit of a warzone these days, to say the least, although it will always be home to me in some capacity. Although

I like to think it's my warzone, it has become a bit reckless. This moment is one I will never forget, and actual proof of the supernatural power of something far bigger than ourselves. While walking a route that has become routine to me, crossing 36th Street between First and Second Avenue, I looked to my right like I always do. I will yield to traffic if there is any, and on this particular day at this moment, as I turn my head to the right there is a blue car speeding literally right at me. At the moment I saw it, it was roughly two feet away. At that moment I said to myself one thing. We are not getting out of this; how do we minimize the damage? I braced myself and put my right arm out, with the intention that if I got run over or flipped over this car and landed on my head, this human experience could come to an end, but if my arm got annihilated, I could potentially recover from that. Bang! The car drove right into me. As it hit me, I spun around to the direction I was heading and the car also grazed my hip, took off, and sped away, going through two consecutive red lights and was gone. I was in a bit of shock at that moment, my arm banged up and a bit bloody. I continued to walk up 36th Street for a couple of moments when a big truck stopped at a red light near me and rolled down their window. A guy yells out "Holy s**t, are you okay, man? That was an incredible spin move. That jerk hit you then went through two red lights, call the cops!" I checked out my arm, which, although immediately bloody and bruised, seemed to have avoided major damage. I did call the cops to report the guy and also get medically checked out.

This incident really rocked me for a couple of days. The crazy part of this story is this. In that very brief moment when I saw the car coming right at me, there was no panic. I wasn't scared. The reason being is because of my faith and relationship with God and my belief that I am always being protected and propelled. I responded instead of reacting, which is another great life lesson perhaps to be discussed later on. When I vulnerably chose to discuss this near-death experience to my community on both social media and the CLS Experience podcast, people were blown away. The majority of the consensus was that it was a very close call and I am very blessed to have walked away relatively unscathed. Just to be clear, the car didn't *almost hit me*; the car *drove right into me*. Now what do you think really happened here that enabled me to walk away with very minor bruises and cuts? I think it's safe to say that indeed I was very blessed at this moment, but the truth is this was divine intervention in real time. I believe the work I'm here to do, my assignment if you will, is much bigger. Had that moment been the end of my run here, there would be no Reinvention Formula to help inspire, motivate, and elevate millions of people.

Before I worked on my faith, I used to be that cat who never received blessings. I'd never get "lucky," and I lived in a world in which I was the result of outside circumstances or events. Now, after cultivating a bulletproof faith and relationship with God, I expect the best, and with God's help I will attain the best, or so I choose to believe. It is indeed a fact that those who think with positive self-reliance and strong optimism do tend to manifest the condition they draw upon.

As for the fallout of the hit and run, the NYPD were unable to locate the driver and the cameras from the building near the incident were obstructed by parked cars. They also said, based on where the city is now, even if the guy confessed, there would be minimal consequences. That was disturbing to hear but it also provided me with a bit of closure. Physically I was good to go; however, I did struggle for a couple of weeks emotionally, spiritually, and psychologically. It's interesting to digest. You may think upon reading this, "Wow, Craig is unstoppable or a superhero," and think that I must feel immortal. The truth is yes, I felt a sense of gratitude like never before, but the fascinating part to me was just how mortal I truly felt. Most of the time we're just going through our day and routines and never really come close to a situation where you feel just how fragile life is. This moment was surreal for me. The fact that, just like that, life could be over provided feelings I had never quite experienced before. You would think a moment like this would make you reconsider some things in your life such as career or relationship. Interestingly enough, my career and my relationship with my fiancée are beautiful and in complete alignment with who I am and becoming. However, the experience caused me to reevaluate the people and things I choose to participate in. If a situation isn't a "Hell, yes," then it's a "Hell, no" for me. Life is precious and it could all be over in the blink of an eye. We gotta make every single second count. No more saying yes to things that do not make me feel good.

This incident also made me become hyperfocused on being present and mindful in each and every activity I participate in. From a keynote speech I'm giving, to a coaching call, to a gym session, and all the way to my quality time with my family. I never want to be in a moment and mentally elsewhere. I choose to stack magical and mindful moments now and treat every single encounter like it could be the last. This is a complete paradigm shift with the word *scarcity*, which I speak about with my friend Ed Mylett,[1] global speaker and super entrepreneur, on *The CLS Experience*. What if you treat every single moment as though you don't know when and if you'd have the opportunity to do this again? That same mindset is why, for my first book—the one you're currently reading—I am treating it as though it could be my last. I'm giving everything I've got to every single word, in every sentence, in every paragraph, in every chapter. Scarcity is valuable with a shift of perspective.

Divine intervention has been a beautiful occurrence for me over the last two years and I challenge you to be open and available for your own divine experiences. I don't believe in coincidences. I believe meeting my fiancée Olesya when I did was divine intervention, and I believe every moment in your life that seems like a curveball is, in fact, happening for you to provide a different opportunity that you may not have anticipated. Believe in yourself and believe in something bigger that creates worlds—the divine. Our big problems won't seem so impossible if we let God handle them. Remember this, as written in the Bible, "We may not always see the effects of our faith, but we can be sure that God honors faithfulness." We must also understand that God may use unexpected sources when communicating to us. Let's be available and willing to investigate, and be open to God's surprises and divine intervention.

Ask Yourself: What do you believe in that's bigger than you?

Note

1. https://podcasts.apple.com/us/podcast/2021-main-event-with-ed-mylett/id1533716044?i=1000546375823

25

One Foot in Front of the Other

Small deeds done are better than great deeds planned.

– Peter Marshall

NONE OF THE methodologies, strategies, or concepts in *The Reinvention Formula* matter if you don't act on it. God will give you the green light, but he won't drive the car for you. God told Moses to stop praying and get moving! Prayers must have a vital place in our lives, but we also need to take action. Sometimes we know what to do, but we pray for more guidance as an excuse to postpone doing it. If we know what we should do, then it's time to get moving. We have all been guilty at some point or another of analysis paralysis. Taking action can seem particularly hard when you're facing a big decision. While some amount of planning, preparation, and deliberation is important, the reality is that taking action, even tiny ones, will have a compounding effect to carry you forward toward and through the big decisions. Sometimes, the reality is that *done* is better than *perfect*. Imagine who Picasso would be, or rather wouldn't be, had he not put paint to canvas.

You have to be focused and take the right kinds of action necessary to move forward. If you feel uncomfortable or stretched, that's good! That's the point. You want to grow into something even more, which means doing and trying more than you were doing or trying yesterday. Be incrementally or massively better in your daily actions. Both will get you further than a standstill. Zig Ziglar once said, "You don't have to be great to start, but you have to start to be great." That quote has been glued to my fridge for the last 10 years. No one was ever amazing in their first game, speaking engagement, business meeting, or on the dance floor for that matter. The fear of the cost of inaction must far outweigh the fear of less than perfect action. Ziglar also said this: "Sometimes you can feel afraid to start something new because you're not as good as the others already doing it. Of course you aren't, and that's okay, but if you don't start playing the game and taking action now, you'll never get to their level of greatness." Think about how true and powerful that is. Imagine I never leaned into CLS and put myself out there and began creating and posting content. Think about all the lives we've changed since then that may not have experienced their breakthroughs. If you're scared to take all this knowledge and apply it, then make it bigger than you. Think of all the people who will breathe different oxygen because you showed up and took inspired action. We all have an assignment. Stop letting the ego convince you to play small and hide your gifts from the world. It's not even about you. It's also none of your business what others think about you, so let's go ahead and totally remove that very common limiting belief.

You know what's sexy? Someone who is comfortable and confident in their own skin, and who shows up authentically taking action and making moves. When you take that first step, the chessboard of life begins to move pieces around to conspire in your favor. The key missing element to the global phenomenon *The Secret* is the necessity to take inspired action toward your intentions and goals. I cannot stress this chapter enough. So much of life, and even the marathons, are a mental game. Step inside the arena and be willing to look silly if need be to create opportunities. Nothing will ever replace action. Even the monks who go to sit and pray and do all their work actually physically go somewhere and take action. You cannot read this book and expect a miracle without being open and available to receive it. Now I acknowledge the action of actually reading this book is a fantastic start. But it must be followed up with inspired action.

At the beginning of this book I asked you to commit to not just being interested in the nuggets, but being committed to the process. Here's the thing. As a global speaker, I speak all over the world, and one thing I consistently see is the self-help or personal-development-event junkies who go to numerous events year after year but they still remain in an unfulfilled situation. You absolutely must take some steps to reinvent your identity. We can agree that just consuming this book is priceless, but if it's not acted on, then it will just remain potential knowledge.

Now let's break it down so it seems a lot less scary. When I started CLS, I knew that as an entrepreneur I would not be scoring touchdowns every single day. However, one thing that I could absolutely guarantee and commit to was achieving daily first downs. For my nonfootball fans out there, let me explain. You may not land the big six- or seven-figure deal every day, or that new client or the big partnership, or the monster breakthrough, but if you marry the process you can definitely do something each day that's considered to be progress.

My intention when I first began, I'm talking about the initial first three months of CLS, was to build awareness and build our community—go into groups on Facebook, engage on Instagram lookalike audiences, enter a mastermind, shake hands, put myself out there. That's something that I can control, and these types of actions compound. Meaning they may not result in a massive amount of revenue coming into your business right away, but by being available, it creates quantitative value. At some point in the not-too-distant future, those connections and relationships most likely will turn into something significant and profitable. Imagine you wanted to get really fit or lose some weight or just reinvent your relationship with looking and feeling better. Perhaps you order a new pair of running shoes. Maybe you open the box and leave them where you can see them at your home. Then the next day you take some impossible-to-fail steps toward this goal. You walk over to the shoes, try them on. Then the next day you put them on and walk around your place to break them in or visualize yourself as taking those bad boys out for a spin. The next day, you put them on, go outside and run a half mile in them. Now you have momentum, which is the hardest thing to get and the easiest thing to lose. These small but powerful and essential steps blossom into consistency and thus lead to the eventual touchdowns. There is no substitute for getting off your butt and taking action. Give yourself permission to be less than perfect and don't ever forget the cost of inaction.

Ask Yourself: What's a small step forward that you can take today to further your desires?

26

Unplugged from the Matrix

There is no spoon.

I REMEMBER SEEING the movie *The Matrix* when I was young and thinking that it was a cool unique science fiction film with some badass action sequences. I always get a kick out of how you can reread the same book or rewatch the same movie in a different season of life and have a totally different mind-blowing experience. *The Matrix* began to become more of a documentary for me than a science fiction film over the years since my introduction to NLP. Let me explain.

There's a part of the film in which Morpheus is training Neo to fulfill the prophecy of him becoming "The One" to help the resistance overcome all their adversaries, and they go to visit the extremely wise and future-seeing Oracle. While Neo is waiting to see her (the Oracle) he sees a bunch of special and gifted children utilizing their gifts in the waiting area. There was this boy who was bending a spoon with his mind and this scene actually changed the course of my life. Let's take a look.

The spoon is a metaphor for obstacles in our lives. Initially, Neo believes that the spoon exists in reality and it's not possible to bend it. When he is told that the spoon is just a computer code and part of the Matrix, clarity draws upon him. He is then able to bend the spoon. In the same way we have to realize that obstacles, troubles, and difficulties are just a fragment of our imagination. Once we realize this, then there are no obstacles. We are the masters of our brains and no obstacle is big enough to stop us from achieving our dreams and goals, provided we have the right attitude! In other words the boy is telling Neo not to bend the spoon, but for him to bend himself. All the obstacles are illusions that we as society have created to keep us in this system full of limitations and certain rules. Now I am not alluding to the fact that there shouldn't be rules, but what I am suggesting is that we should question the rules and begin to bend the way we look at certain things. This changes the game because now we are searching for a different positive perspective instead of staying stuck with certain constraints and limitations.

We're about to get really deep. To control your life is to take responsibility for yourself. To assign your life's responsibilities to other external forces would simply empower those forces to take responsibility over your life. Simply put, if you do not control your own life, someone else will do it for you. There is no spoon! This was the most important lesson for Neo played by Keanu Reeves. It helped him realize that manipulating the Matrix wasn't about focusing on objects or trying to force them to chance. His epiphany was seeing that the constraints on what he could accomplish (and the spoon itself) existed nowhere but in his own mind. In order for him to have any control on the world around him, he had to look inward. It was all in his head after all. This whole scene changed my entire perspective and map of the world.

This is the realization that we must look inward to accomplish our goals. We can't change the obstacles, people, or world around us. We shouldn't even blame others of the world itself, for that bears no factor in moving forward. We can only exact control over that which is in our own dominion. The key to the future is all in our heads. So the next time you find yourself in a rough situation, just remember that there is no magic red pill solution. Sometimes you have to let go of your own personal dogma, stop clinging to what is familiar in order to move forward. Also, you should absolutely use the guidance of coaches and mentors, but they can't ever do the life changing for you. You have to walk through the door. And lastly, always remember: There is no spoon! Bend yourself.

Ask Yourself: By bending, what new perspective shows up?

27

Disappointment and Heartbreak

We must accept finite disappointment, but never lose infinite hope.
— Martin Luther King, Jr.

THOSE WHO REALLY live, know the unsettling feeling of disappointment and getting your heart cracked wide open. It's a prerequisite for life that taking big swings will leave you open to experiencing big misses. The alternative is that you don't put yourself out there much and just coast in your comfort zone and exist, but then quite possibly you won't experience as much disappointment because you have very low expectations and exposure to coming up short. That's the mentality of not even being alive much. When a setback occurs in life—perhaps a small obstacle or a heartbreaking crushing defeat—you don't have to approve of it, but you absolutely must accept it. Acceptance opens the door for the dance of self-forgiveness.

The best way I know to handle disappointment is by forgiving yourself and taking accountability and ownership for the situation, even if in retrospect it wasn't truly your fault. Own it. Assume massive responsibility for everything that happens because this elevates you to a position of power where you are in control of your life, to the best of your ability. When my team of employees comes up short or makes an error, I automatically go to bat for them and ask myself how I could have possibly communicated the task at hand more effectively. This way I am constantly looking for ways to improve and get better as a leader and as an all-around human. Now, back to heartbreak.

It's perfectly normal to struggle with and feel overwhelmed by disappointment. Give yourself grace and be kind to yourself. I cannot stress this enough. Practice being kind to yourself and don't put yourself into a downward spiral. It's been said that one way to handle disappointment is to adjust your expectations. I don't know if I entirely agree with this. I think you should think and play big in life. Maintain the mindset that as you continue to think and play much bigger in the world, coming up short from time to time is a part of the game. Can we grow from the disappointment? Can we learn why we came up short, can we practice gratitude for the experience and adjust our strategies while being kind to ourselves? I say yes.

The most important thing to extract from the feelings of heartbreak and disappointment is to not let the feelings linger. Try not to focus on your negative emotions for a long period of time. Take some time to process and adjust. However, spending too much time and energy on your disappointment will have a damaging effect on your frequency or emotional state as well as your mental health. Let's be aware and acknowledge but not suffer. Let's identify positive strategies to ensure that you don't dwell in a bubble of negativity. Self-talk and positive mantras can be super effective as well as journaling and having a support system to keep you elevated. I want to be clear, I am not suggesting that you mask and numb the moments that break your heart. What I am saying is the best of the best have strategies and processes to handle these life turbulences and take proactive steps forward. Maybe you need to meditate, or go for a run, or take time to allow all the feelings to come through you. Ask yourself powerful questions about what happened, and adjust for next time. After you give yourself that grace, absolutely get back in the game.

After my first marathon in New York, I was disappointed that I failed to break the benchmark of a sub-four-hour race. It stung and it was a bitter pill to swallow. I also knew that there was significant room for improvement, which was exciting. I licked my wounds, I researched how to get faster, build stamina, and becme a master of nutrition. It took me two more attempts to finally break that sub-four-hour marathon, and now that I look back, that journey was so special because I made no excuses and I handled it with grace and continued to get back in the game. Running a marathon is typically not life or death, and there are much bigger heartbreaks that may punch us in the gut. For example, finding out I had a tumor in my foot was disappointing and I certainly allowed myself to feel disappointed; however, I took all those strong feelings and transferred that energy to my recovery and what I could take advantage of while being immobile for months. Getting hit by a speeding car that didn't even stop to see if I was okay and then took off definitely shook me up and created some emotional trauma for a bit. I didn't approve of that incident, but I did accept it and decided to focus on the positives from that near-death experience—being alive, being protected, becoming more mindful and present. There is always a choice in life. The lockdown at the beginning of the pandemic provided me with a choice: Netflix and alcohol, or work on myself and explore my purpose and double down on my mental fitness. I am not suggesting heartbreak is easy, but I am saying there is always a choice. Self-forgiveness is huge for being in the position you're in. Take pride in how you handle the tough situations in life.

Sometimes we get our hearts cracked wide open with a divorce or a breakup. I know it hurts badly. I have been there myself when a long-term relationship ends. That season of life is always gut wrenching. Take some time to journal about all the positives that occurred while in the relationship and what you learned about yourself. Perhaps the relationship you thought would be your last was really identifying what's truly in alignment with who you are and who you are becoming. Now you have priceless data to become better and show up wiser, more battle tested, and available for the correct partner. I know when I had gotten out of a relationship years back, I learned so much about myself from that experience that it made me more authentic and clear about who I am and who I eventually wanted to settle down with. I became a vibrational match for the right person, also known as Olesya. Until my previous breakup, I didn't realize what was truly important to me in a partner. I am so grateful for the relationships that didn't work out because I gained so much information and data and created a better version of myself in the process. Don't ever lose hope in life. Life will indeed crack your heart wide open and you will hurt, and then you will hurt a little less, and eventually you will heal. You will be better for it and more available for the right things or people in alignment with who you are and who you are becoming.

Sometimes we suffer a major blow with the death of a loved one. I know this can rock your world, because as I have experienced it and also seen how others experience it as well. First and foremost, under-stand that life isn't always fair, sometimes the unimaginable happens and you find yourself asking lots of questions and feeling down and out of the fight. Look, I get it. Take time to grieve. Allow the emotions to flow. Find relief in exercise, supportive people, journaling, or however you choose to go through the pain. Use this time to even strengthen your relationship with God or whoever and whatever you believe in. Transform your relationship with the one who is gone. Embrace that they are still with you but in a different capacity. Talking about these moments is helpful and should not be bottled up. Acceptance and hope are the key to moving forward. It's your race, your pace but, at your pace, keep moving forward. That's the key to life. Honor your lost loved ones by living authentically and making every second count.

Some of you are simply in a season of disappointment for just not being where you had planned or hoped to be at this part of your life. Two words. Reinvention Season. Forgive yourself, be kind and accept where you are and take one small step at a time in a forward direction. The power of understanding that acceptance doesn't mean approval, allows you some grace, but it also cements the underlying strategy to continue to exercise hope, self-forgiveness, and the ability to build resilience and keep moving forward. When you adopt the mindset that a life worth living always comes with a price of inevitable setbacks and misses, you can embrace them as a part of the journey and fall in love with the process—the beautiful and abundant, as well as the heartbreaks and disappointments. You only lose if you quit. No one said life was going to be easy, I am just saying that it will all be worth it, if you step into alignment and live with intention and continue to open your heart.

Humans tend to punish themselves continuously with no end in sight for not being where they believe they should be. No one abuses or is harder on us than we are on ourselves. Exercise kindness and self-forgiveness and transfer your energy to what happens next in a positive and productive way that sets you up for success for the future. Trust me; disappointment and heartbreak won't ever fully go away, so it's best to get good at handling them and becoming a master of how to transform those feelings to work for you and not against you.

Ask Yourself: What disappointment or heartbreak did you overcome?

28

Purpose

Those who have a "why" to live, can bear with almost any "how."

— Viktor E. Frankl

THE MEANING OF life may not only differ from one person to another, but each of us may have a different life purpose at each season of life. The important thing is for each goal or objective to give us purpose and encouragement to get up in the morning and fight for what we want. The best way to avoid a burnout and stay enthusiastic and excited about life is to have a particular reason for getting up every morning. What is your mission, what keeps you in the fight when the inevitable setback occurs? What is the idea that you are inspired by, that gets you up after getting punched in the gut? What keeps you going when you're feeling tired and you just don't have the energy on a given day? Why are you here?

Viktor Frankl lived through the horrors of the Holocaust, a prisoner in Auschwitz and Dachau. The loss of his family clarified for him that his purpose in this world was simply to help others find their own purpose in life. This man had lost nearly everything important and dear to his heart, but he cultivated his assignment and meaning and was able to persevere. He wrote one of the most influential books of all time called *Man's Search for Meaning*. In it, he discusses how there is nothing worse than perceiving that our suffering is useless. However, if you can find a purpose, you won't just endure your suffering; you'll see it as a challenge. Now, I'm not suggesting that everyone is here to suffer. However, if you identify your purpose and assignment first, then the inevitable obstacles, challenges, and adversity will not cause suffering because your *why* will always be stronger than your *how*.

When I found myself in my darkest season of life a few years back, when it seemed like it was a struggle just to get up in the morning, I didn't have a clear purpose or meaning. I wasn't passionate about my job at the time, I wasn't in alignment with the people around me, and I lacked inspiration because there was no clear obvious path. I was going through the motions and was consumed with emotional and spiritual pain. Once I started running marathons, I became inspired. I was constantly working on myself and who I needed to become to be the type of cat who runs marathons and runs them well. Running became my purpose for a season, which helped me become a better version of myself. Eventually it led me to become available to give birth to CLS. For anyone right now struggling to find meaning, a short-term purpose can make all the difference in getting your spark back. Once the flame is lit, it begins to grow and your frequency begins to elevate, creating a higher vibration for you to identify what your song and dance are. The absence of a real purpose in life is the number-one missing link that I have observed in people who struggle with their mental health.

A vision or a goal will keep someone alive when nothing else will. I have witnessed it with my own father. At the time of his cancer diagnosis, he was given a very pessimistic outlook. What the doctors didn't take into consideration was my dad's unwavering desire to watch his kids grow, his grandson come into this world, his future daughter-in-law Olesya become part of the family, and the rise of CLS, which has captivated his heart with enormous pride and joy. This is my dad's meaning in the face of adversity in the form of cancer. My dad keeps fighting and is the strongest person I have ever met, and I take full responsibility for keeping him excited and engaged with all the wonderful developments we have going on, such as the publication of our first book, *The Reinvention Formula*.

All the answers to our questions of life are not on the outside. Books will not explain to us what our true meaning is nor will our family or friends. All our desires, goals, passions, and meanings are within us, and they may change over the course of different seasons of life as we evolve and spread our wings. Every second of every single day is an opportunity to make a decision that will determine whether we will be a victim of circumstance or if we will act with true authenticity and integrity, listening to our own true self. About a decade ago when I was a bit more unenlightened, I was motivated by money and sought validation through my financial success. That was immature, but I was young and not anywhere close to where I am today spiritually. However, money inspired me back then. I'm not suggesting that it was the correct purpose, but it was one nevertheless. Today I am driven by impact, contribution, and happiness, which all happen to include

CLS, so I am very grateful and blessed. It took me a while and some really dark seasons, but I never gave up or lost hope that I would be able to eventually tap into my assignment, my meaning, and my purpose. Better late than never is the understatement of my lifetime. Since identifying my life mission to help others identify and pursue their own potential, my life has resembled a rocket ship over the last two years in my career, relationships, finances, fitness, spirituality, happiness, and overall quality of life. Let's say, "Hell, yes" to life and agree to never give up on finding our true authentic purpose here on this beautiful yet very short human experience.

Ask Yourself: Why are you here?

29

There Are No Rules

Life is a beautiful, weird, and crazy journey that continues to get better with every moment that you double down on yourself and step into alignment with your soul's purpose.

– Craig Siegel

FOR THOSE READING this and who may be in a later season of life right now, know this. I remember thinking in my 20s that 40 was old. And in my early 30s I thought if you didn't make it yet, it wouldn't happen, ever. Now I am here to tell you that life keeps getting richer. The more you keep doing the inner work and showing up for yourself, the more available you become for the moments that take your breath away. You possess the power to do literally anything you want or desire in this life. As we speak, I am shedding old skin, beliefs, and identities and cultivating a new profound understanding around the meaning of infinite possibilities.

What you believe and what you allow yourself to consume, you become. So if you don't like the story you wake up telling yourself day after day . . . change it. Rewrite the script and fill yourself up with the things that elevate you, lift you up, and make you feel like you could actually *fly*. Because you can. You cannot tell me otherwise. If you want it badly enough, you will. Chase the butterflies. To any of you out there who think you are too old or too young to do something you always wanted to do, the only thing holding you back is *you* and that limited way of thinking. Here's to aligning our actions to meet those intentions so we can continue to make every single one of our deepest intentions a living breathing reality. It's time to become congruent with our aligned actions and intentions.

Each of us may create a different model of the world we share and thus come to live in a somewhat different reality. As we discussed in "The Power of Neuro-Linguistic Programming (NLP)," Chapter 19, our model of reality, rather than reality itself, is what will determine how we will act and perform. The very awareness of this concept is the difference between someone who thinks at 50 that they're done, and the person who thinks at 60 that they are just getting warmed up. On our episode on *The CLS Experience*, Hollywood juggernaut Frank Grillo[1] said that he got what society would consider to be a late start in his

Hollywood career, receiving his big break in the movie *Warrior* in his 40s. Since that pivotal moment in his career, he's gone on to star in several of Marvel's *Captain America* films, the *Purge* franchise, *Zero Dark Thirty*, the hit show *Billions* and many more. His life has become more abundant as he gets older. The better it gets, the better it gets. Why? Because he knows that there are no rules. Forty doesn't mean you're old, and 20 doesn't mean you're young. It's about what you believe to be possible for you at this moment in your life, regardless of what has been the standard to this point. The legendary Henry Ford said, "Whether you think you can, or you think you can't—you're right."

Let's unpack that because I think it's pivotal for your life's work. If you feel defeated, then you are. If you feel abundant and available, then you are. I was available for reinvention at 35 and I lived more the previous 2 years than the previous 35 combined. I believed I had a mission, a resourceful and determined maniacal drive, and the positive attitude to push through during the season of grind.

There's a Craig in an alternative quantum universe who didn't think he could reinvent himself. He went back to Wall Street after the lockdown and died a slow death of unhappiness, unfulfillment, and lack of purpose and meaning, leading to poor choices and sadness. I am so proud of this Craig, for acting on that 20 seconds of courage and cosigning abundance and possibilities. My family and readers, reinvention is ready when you are. It is never too late unless you refuse to remove the scarcity and replace it with the most powerful question possible: What could go right? Let's explore that, let's cosign that and raise our hand for all that potential and opportunity. You are here for a reason, and it is your responsibility to identify what that is, double down on your authentic inspiration, and contribute to the world. Own that and embrace it. After all, there is only one you. The world needs you to step into your power. Ya dig?

Ask Yourself: Where have you been stuck trying to abide by what you think are the typical rules based on society?

Note

1. https://podcasts.apple.com/us/podcast/2022-main-event-with-frank-grillo/id1533716044?i=1000591440724

30

Back on the Board

We can choose gratitude, and while that doesn't take away our pain during hard times, it can give us a fresh perspective.

– Bethany Hamilton

THERE'S A MESSAGE in everything, if you're available to identify it. As a movie guy, I have my go-to films that I throw on repeatedly for inspiration and during challenging seasons of life. I highly suggest that you begin to cultivate a list of movies that elevate your state. I'm obsessed with the movie *Soul Surfer*, based on a true story about professional surfer Bethany Hamilton,[1] who, after losing her arm to a shark attack, bounced back and went on to have a very successful pro career and an even more impactful career as a speaker, author, and beacon of hope, courage, and inspiration for millions. When I started CLS she was on the white board of guests I had to connect with to share her powerful story on *The CLS Experience*, where she pulled back the curtain and dropped many priceless raw truth bombs.

I really connected with Bethany years back when I found myself unhappy and searching for meaning. I had been through some things including a toxic relationship, bad investments, my father's cancer diagnosis, and a lack of true purpose. Bethany stands for hope, faith, and gratitude. Her attitude is truly remarkable and something special and contagious. I have since read her book and watched the movie an abundance of times and it always elevates me. Connecting with her for the podcast was so special, because I really wanted to thank her face to face for sharing her unbelievable story with such strength and courage, which made a huge impact on me.

After Bethany lost her arm to a shark attack, she never stayed in the victim mentality. She stayed really positive, which, I imagine, would have been tough for a young girl to do after having her whole life turned upside down in the blink of an eye. She was motivated to get right back in the water after she healed, did not accept anyone feeling sorry for her, and believed that even though she didn't know it at the time, God had much bigger plans for her in this world. I imagine it's safe to say that from this life-altering experience, she has made a much,

much bigger impact on the world than if she just kept surfing with two arms, and didn't have this huge adversity that she had to overcome.

Bethany chose gratitude. You see, here's the thing about the super-power that is gratitude. You can't be a victim and be grateful at the same time. You can't be miserable and grateful at the same time. The frequency of gratitude is so strong that it trumps negative feelings if you choose it. I remember during my pity party season of life, that after seeing Bethany's story and most importantly her unbelievably positive attitude toward life adversity, it rubbed off on me. It gave me perspective. Here is Bethany, losing an arm to a shark attack and rather than choosing a negative attitude, which no one would have faulted her for, she chose gratitude when it was toughest to choose. As a result, she looked at this whole situation with a fresh perspective, choosing to believe that this happened *for* her and not *to* her. As a result, she can now inspire millions of people by showing that she is qualified to speak on overcoming challenges while maintaining a positive attitude. If she can choose to be thankful that she didn't die, and now has an opportunity to inspire the world, there has got to be a different perspective that *we* can choose as well, especially during tough seasons.

Gratitude is a choice and it's a superpower. When you start being grateful for all the things you have instead of bitter about the things you don't have, you elevate your frequency and begin to be positive. I'm grateful for my tumor season because it helped me slow down a bit, dive into my spirituality, and cultivate an understanding of the quantum and energy fields. And most importantly, it provided me with a new opportunity to run the NYC Marathon to inspire my dad and raise thousands of dollars for the American Cancer Society.

Life will throw you a curve ball when you're anticipating a fast ball, but with the mindset that it's happening *for* us, to protect and propel us to something much greater, then essentially, we become unstoppable. Gratitude is pausing to notice and appreciate what we often take for granted, such as having the ability to read this book.

There are many ways to practice gratitude and make it part of your lifestyle, which will change everything for you. Begin to be intentional about noticing good things in your life. Whenever you're in a lowered emotional state or frequency, pause and list five things that you're currently grateful for. Immediately your vibration will elevate and you will show up more powerful, magnetic, and open to abundance. Remember, and I can't stress this enough, if you choose gratitude, you're also choosing to be positive and remove negativity from your life.

For those that find this hard to do, I challenge you to practice being grateful for literally everything that you have in your life for 24 hours. Watch how you elevate your entire physiology and begin to attract more abundance into your life. After the 24 hours is up, you have my permission to reevaluate if you want to continue to practice gratitude moving forward. I have yet to see anyone choose to go back to their old lifestyle of victim mentality and negative emotions. Gratitude is a game changer and it's totally free; all you have to do is commit and begin to shift your perspective to the things you are thankful for. Why wait until Thanksgiving? Start today with shifting your entire perspective and watch how you are no longer at the mercy of life circumstances and obstacles.

One of the concepts that Bethany illustrates so beautifully in her message is the combination of gratitude and faith. Some of the notes I took while reading and listening to her story are worth mentioning. For anyone currently going through a tough season right now, these will certainly hit home. You can and will get through it. God will never leave you or forsake you. The past is the past; on to bigger and better things. Life is full of "what if's." You can't let it hold you back. In her case, the "what if" was: What if she hadn't gone surfing the day of the shark attack? If you ask yourself "what if" you're not really living at all; you're just kinda going through the motions with no meaning. The only thing that will never go away, will never fail you, is your faith in God.

Just reading some of my notes from journaling on Bethany's story immediately elevates me. They get me feeling an unwavering sense of gratitude and perspective. One of my favorite lines in the film is when Bethany decides that she is going to compete again after losing her arm and her dad is telling her it's going to be tough. Bethany responds with,

"I don't need easy, I just need possible." This line gives me chills. It's such a beautiful metaphor for life. We have an imagination, and what we believe we can achieve, no matter how potentially difficult it may be. I just love this message. Additionally, Bethany says, "Courage doesn't mean you don't get afraid. Courage means you don't let fear stop you." How powerful is that? Courage is what life's all about, feeling the fear and pushing through anyway. It's the same reason I fell in love with running marathons.

The all-time greats whom I have had the honor of having on the CLS Experience podcast and becoming friends with all tend to have a lot of courage. You see most people shy away from fear. Life doesn't always get easier, but we can get stronger. By reading *The Reinvention Formula*, one of my hopes is that you have cultivated a bulletproof mindset and you have begun to lean into scary but exhilarating situations, knowing that on the other side massive growth awaits. Embrace that. Change your perspective. Bethany mentions, "Fear is something that can really hold us all back from different things in life. It's important to notice what your fears are and try to conquer them." My family, listen here as we close this chapter with a quote from Bethany about shifting your perspective: "Gratitude is a theme in my life. Appreciation is how I was able to quickly shift my mindset after losing my arm. Instead of focusing on what I didn't like about my body or my limitations, I choose to be grateful for the remarkable body that I have."

We all have moments in our lives that seem negative or we don't have answers about why they happened. However, we can choose a different perspective, one of gratitude. Realizing that we are not alone in this world, and that we are always being protected and propelled is the antidote to fear crippling victim mentality. Whether it's surfing, business, heartbreak, or anything in between, always get back on the board.

Ask Yourself: What are three things that you are grateful for right now?

Note

1. https://podcasts.apple.com/us/podcast/back-on-the-board-with-bethany-hamilton/id1533716044?i=1000541175905

31

Vulnerability Is a Superpower

Vulnerability sounds like truth and feels like courage. Truth and courage aren't always comfortable, but they're never weakness.

— Brené Brown

BACK IN THE day when I was growing up, being vulnerable, especially for a man, was considered to be weak. Especially for a man sharing his feelings, it became a sign of a lack of masculinity. Still to this day we are seeing way too many people, who appear to be very happy and have it all together on the outside, take their own lives. I want to do my part and embrace and encourage talking about what's really going on. I'm not a doctor and I don't have all the cures for depression and anxiety, but I do know this. Talking about what's really going on to the right person in the right environment can help a great deal. We are all going through something in some capacity. Some have better ways of concealing it. I always thought it was interesting that if you go on social media and see someone's life highlight reel on their feed, it looks like they couldn't be happier or more on fire. Next thing you know they're going through a divorce. It's okay to not be okay. What's not okay is avoiding talking through it and asking for help.

One thing that I really have worked on a lot since becoming a public figure is to embrace vulnerability and show up as the most real, most authentic version of myself. I remember performing a keynote speech in Dallas with Ryan Serhant from Bravo's *Million Dollar Listing* less than a week after getting hit by a car. I was still processing the event and wasn't 100% myself. The first thing I did when I took the stage was open up like a flower and let everyone know about the incident, and that I am still going through the emotional trauma, but it's important that I turn that into a lesson and be there in Dallas to elevate and inspire others. By showing up that way, the audience was on the edge of their seats for the entire performance, and nearly everyone came up to me after and thanked me for the radical honesty and courage to still perform and let them in. They told me I stole the show. I'd like to believe we would have stolen the show anyway (this is where I'd insert a winking emoji). All kidding aside, when you have the courage to show your hand, the good and the ugly, you cultivate real power by releasing the expectation of anyone who may or may not judge you. If you can be honest when things are not so pretty, people will love, respect, and gravitate toward you because they will be able to relate. It shows that all of us are human, but it's how we handle the tough moments that turns courage into vulnerability.

Now I should add a disclaimer that not everyone will love your raw vulnerability, but I challenge you to not care what the wrong people think of you. Notice how I didn't say that you shouldn't care what anyone thinks. It's become trendy to say I don't care what anyone thinks, especially from haters on social media. That part I agree with. However, we are neurologically wired to care what people think. Just make sure you care what the right people think. Studies show you measure courage by how vulnerable you are willing to be. How cool is that? Practice being vulnerable and you'll begin to cultivate courage, one of the most important life characteristics anyone can possess. Where I used to have a certain narrow-minded perspective regarding being vulnerable, I have now leaned into it and begun to associate it with pleasure, because I know every time I show up, whether to tell the CLS audience that a tumor was discovered in my foot or that I was hit by a car in a hit-and-run, I have the ability to help someone who also may be going through a hard season to let them know they are not alone, and we can choose optimism in the face of adversity.

When I was growing up, I was a superhero and comic book nerd. Who am I kidding, I am still very much a superhero geek. Arguably the most well known superhero is and was Superman. Sure he's cool, but I could never relate to him or connect with his story. Essentially, he's an alien who is beyond powerful and although he does have his kryptonite, for the most part it's tough to be able to resonate with him. For me personally, Batman was my guy. He was a human who was extremely skilled in martial arts and known as the world's best detective. I connected with him because in my head, that was attainable. He could very well get his ass kicked, and the stakes were high because he was a human who was a great crime fighter but also had some vulnerability. Why am I sharing this story? People connect with people who are relatable. They want to be able to feel a sense of connection. The more I show up raw and open for my community, the stronger the connection we build. Vulnerability is not a weakness. On the contrary, it's a superpower, and if you choose that mindset, watch how the world begins to gravitate toward you. Of course there will be a portion of your audience, customers, or friends who flock away. Good, we are not everyone's glass of whiskey so let's stop pretending to be.

I had a conversation with my good friend Dr. Caroline Leaf[1] on her show and then shared it with our audience as well on *The CLS Experience*. We got deep below the surface, and I think this conversation was massive for the world. Let's say you had a day—possibly a crappy day—or you faced some challenges or obstacles. When you come home, it's okay to show your children that you're not in the best frequency due to your tough day, but then, show your children how you handle this moment. In other words, you were upset or at a lower frequency, but you made the choice to not dwell there and you do the work to transform from reactive to proactive and choose a positive outlook with the understanding that not every day is a 10 out of 10. Life won't always be sunshine and rainbows—for instance, getting a tumor diagnosis in my foot while I'm training for the Chicago Marathon, or getting hit by a car in a hit-and-run, or even having your best friend in the world, in this case my father, getting diagnosed with cancer. What I've learned so far is that showcasing these challenging life moments, and then, more importantly, displaying how I handle these disappointments is what connects and inspires people around me. Additionally, courage and resilience are muscles that you can strengthen with reps and practice. Let's agree that vulnerability creates courage and that helps both ourselves and the people around us.

Ask Yourself: How can you practice vulnerability right now?

Note

1. https://podcasts.apple.com/us/podcast/near-death-experiences-with-dr-caroline-leaf/id1533716044?i=1000590339333

32

Falling in Love

You know you're in love when you can't fall asleep because reality is finally better than your dreams.

— Dr. Seuss

THIS CHAPTER HAS dual meanings, so grab your tissues and let's get deep—real deep. A few years back after getting out of a toxic relationship and choosing to stay stuck at a job that did not light up my soul, I had a different definition of the word *love* than I do now. We're going to talk about falling in love with another human, your career, and most importantly, how to fall in love with yourself first.

For years, back on Wall Street, I lost my smile. I was miserable at my career, and my relationship with my girlfriend at the time felt very wrong for many reasons. I want to be clear I am not pointing fingers, because a lot of it was my fault, and we weren't the best fit for each other. I had gotten out of shape, and for someone who worked out in some capacity for 15 years I had let myself go a bit to say the least. I was drinking more alcohol than I'd like to admit to escape and numb my reality. I was out of alignment in many ways. But then something happened. I began to sharpen the ax again—more specifically, in my journal. I started to reflect on where I was at, and I practiced forgiveness for myself for not being in the position I thought I might have been at this time, and I started to give myself some grace. I started to become available little by little to reinvent myself although I was still far away from Craig 2.0 and CLS.

By choosing to love myself again and replace bitterness and regret with self-love and opportunities, running found me. I was available. The reason why I am so romantic about running is because running helped me love myself again. It gave me a purpose, it was challenging but achievable, and it also helped me get into the best physical shape of my life, which, in my opinion, is a reflection of how much you respect yourself. I began to love, respect, and believe in myself again. Based on my life experience you have to go through the dark seasons to want to see the light.

This moment in my life was massive. I started to fall in love with myself and I cultivated purpose, grace, and quadrupled down on my

154

relationship with God. You probably thought I was going to dive into talking about my fiancée with the title of this chapter, and I will, but before you can create a life to die for you must practice self-love. Whatever skeletons you may have in your closet, whatever you have been through, perhaps abuse, trauma, heartbreak, the death of a loved one, or anything else, you must know two things. First, something much bigger than us loves you and values you more than you can ever imagine, and second, you must love yourself and embrace all your scars and past history of forgettable moments.

Once I began to get excited and love myself again, the ending of my past relationship felt right and in alignment with who I was becoming. I started to shift my mindset. If I really loved and respected myself then I would not choose to be in a relationship that didn't feel right for me. It's a normal emotion for people coming out of relationships to think they will never find the right one or that love just isn't in the cards for them. Having begun to grow and evolve, what worked for me at this season was divorcing myself from the outcome and expectations and doubling down on working on myself to become the best version of myself so that I could become available for the right partner at some point who was in alignment with this version of Craig. That was a Craig who loved and respected himself. More to come on this shortly.

Now that we've discussed falling in love with yourself, the great, the ugly, and everything in between, it's time to fall in love with your purpose or your career. Statistics show that you will spend one-third of your life in your career. Some say that's 90,000 hours, depending on what you do and how long you have in this human experience. Think about that for a moment. 90,000 hours will be allocated to your career. You better love it! For me personally, when I was in my season of darkness, a lot of it was caused by getting myself in a position where I wasn't happy in my career and, as a result, I ended up coming home at night depleted. This causes so many toxic and negative emotions.

When I became ready and available to create something that I both loved and that I felt would be a contribution to the world, CLS was born. Trust me, when you go all in on your passions and you're willing to hustle and grind for a season, you can absolutely figure out how to monetize it. You cannot convince me otherwise. Adding value gets you rich and it lights up your soul. At the risk of this chapter being a trigger for some, I feel it's my responsibility to let you know that if you are in a career that doesn't light you up or make you a good income, you're choosing to stay comfortable and stuck.

The truth is you can do anything you want in this world, especially with the limitless information now at your fingertips from the Internet, YouTube, books, and podcasts, and, quite frankly, the ability to reach out for help. There is no excuse to not be able to cultivate the information you need to pursue a career that makes you happy. You better start thinking about falling in love with your career. We don't get a sequel for this life, at least not in this human experience, so go out there and do heartfelt fulfilling work.

The irony is when you commit to falling in love with your career, more doors will open and opportunities will present themselves. Is it possible to fall in love with the job you currently have and learn to love it? Yes, I believe you can, but if it doesn't have you doing a triple backflip into a split out of bed most days, then just maybe you're not really in love with it. Look, I totally understand that not everyone is here to make a massive impact on the world, and for some just being an amazing wife or mom is priority number one. And let me be clear, there is probably no more important job than being a mother. Entrepreneur and co-founder of billion-dollar juggernaut Quest Nutrition Lisa Bilyeu[1] and I had this exact conversation on *The CLS Experience*. You better have some hobbies or passions to pursue along with this to keep your soul lit and in love with yourself or after the kids have grown, perhaps consider what you want to do for your next season of life. Just make sure that you are happy and your purpose is strong and you're in love with your life. A career will play a massive role in your life and you want to love it, trust me on this.

Okay, fine. Let's get a little mushy. So reflecting on this chapter, we discussed how I started to love myself again, priority number one, then I began to create a career that I loved. My life was full of love and I lived with my heart wide open. When I was least expecting it, once I was available, I met Olesya.

You attract what you are. I'm a big believer in that. It can be triggering or it can be liberating, depending on your perspective. If you're willing to surrender and flow, you have an opportunity to improve and work on yourself in order to attract a better life for yourself. I want to be very clear, in my dark seasons of life a few years back, I blamed absolutely no one and took full responsibility and ownership for being exactly where I was. This is powerful, because you can start recreating yourself like clay and shed the old identities that were holding you back.

I began to work on myself and started to become a much better human being. Starting with my habits and my discipline all the way to my personality traits such as becoming more empathetic, humble, and kind. So the old Craig, who was slowly but surely disappearing, was no longer available to attract a person who would gravitate toward that Craig. Are you with me so far? Okay, great. I want to also say that at this time I was not looking for a partner specifically where I would be creating any type of resistance due to forcing it; I was, however, available. Olesya and I met and went for a cup of coffee on Valentines Day 2021. I knew right away that this girl was something different. Clearly she was beautiful and kind, but I was attracted to her soul and her sense of humor, which captivated me. We had both been through some stuff and were both in that season of knowing what we didn't want and working on ourselves and then BANG! We crossed paths and it was game over for me.

It's hard to nail down one important characteristic that takes the cake to create a successful relationship, but one for me that really stands out, based on my time here on earth, is respect. You won't always agree with your partner, and that's perfectly okay, but you absolutely must respect them. Once respect is gone, at least in my opinion, it's hard to recover, and I think this is true in any relationship—business, friendship, or your romantic partner. There has to be a level of mutual respect for one another. Olesya is the most beautiful girl I have ever met, both inside and outside. I love the importance of family to her, her immigrant work ethic, her hilarious sense of humor, her passion for fitness, and her overall selfless and supportive nature for me was the perfect match. While building CLS, especially in the season of grind, it's going to take a special cat to embrace all that comes with this, and she was the perfect co-pilot. I love this girl and it makes waiting a bit later in life to really settle down all worth the wait, because one should never settle for anything less than their highest standard. Olesya far surpassed any relationship expectations that I ever had. Lesson time: it's a great season of life to be single, to work on yourself, and to explore life. Don't ever settle. When you know, you know.

I proposed to Olesya in July 2022 in the most beautiful and special fashion in Brooklyn, where she grew up after moving from Ukraine, and I had an abundance of surprises lined up, all of which went off perfectly without a hitch. When does that ever happen, right? Both our families were waiting after she said yes to run out and surprise her, and it was the most magical moment. She was crying, so were both our moms and our dads—both of whom were dealing with some health struggles at the time—who were present and grinning from ear to ear. Our siblings and our immediate family made this the most special moment. As relationship expert and bestselling author John Gray,[2] who wrote the bestselling book of the 1990s *Men Are from Mars, Women Are from Venus*, told me on *The CLS Experience*, you should go the extra mile when it comes to your proposal. Make it special, pull out all the stops. After all, you only plan on doing this once.

The rest is history, the career is building, my co-pilot and my wife to be by my side. There is no going back to my old life. I have shed those old identities and released those old stories, and I am excited to build a life with Olesya while impacting the world. But first, we have to love ourselves before anyone else can truly love us. Own every part of you including the parts you think are ugly, for when you embrace all of you, that is the sexiest and most attractive thing you can do. Own your whole story with confidence. Most importantly, never ever stop working on yourself.

Ask Yourself: What are three things you love about yourself?

Notes

1. https://podcasts.apple.com/us/podcast/goddess-energy-with-lisa-bilyeu/id1533716044?i=1000589963986
2. https://podcasts.apple.com/us/podcast/men-are-from-mars-women-are-from-venus-with-john-gray/id1533716044?i=1000578466790

33

Build Your Own Table

It's pretty simple. If you don't have a seat at the table yet, you have two options. Bring a stool and impose your will, or build a new table.

– Craig Siegel

No ONE SAID life would be easy. There won't always be the perfect career or relationship falling out of the sky into your lap. Often, we have to take what we want, with all due respect. That means if you want something, you have to go get it. I believe that everything can be figured out. Marie Forleo nails this in her book and on our episode on *The CLS Experience*. She says that everything is "figureoutable," and I agree.[1] You can literally create a job at a company that doesn't have a position for you. You can create a product to bring to the market where it may be needed. You have to cultivate that innovative and creative mindset and combine that with maniacal drive.

I've studied the all-time-great innovators across many different industries and arenas. Legends such as Walt Disney, Arnold Schwarzenegger, Vince McMahon, Steve Jobs, James Cameron, Ray Kroc, and Freddie Mercury, just to name a few. I was obsessed with learning what actually makes someone a genius. As it turns out, based on my research, it is the thinking process behind the accomplishment that is the most important element of creating something like genius. It is generally not reality that limits us or empowers us, but rather our map or our perception of reality. The disrupters and trailblazers that I listed have been so effective in changing the world because they possess a map of the world that allows them to perceive the greatest number of available choices and perspectives. A person who is considered a genius then simply just maintains a richer and wider way of organizing, perceiving, and responding to the world. In other words, a strategy is like a program on a computer. It tells you what to do with the information you are getting, and just like a computer program, you can use the same strategy to process a lot of different kinds of information and knowledge.

Furthermore, all geniuses have a well-developed ability to visualize. Walt Disney once said, "I must explore and experiment . . . I resent the limits of my own imagination." I mean, how powerful is that.

This reminds me of some of the characteristics of P. T. Barnum from "The Greatest Showman," Chapter 16, earlier in this book. Look what that guy created. You see, here's the thing. This chapter should have you very excited and exhilarated about what's possible for you. That means that you don't have to be born with a really high IQ to be considered a genius. It is the strategy that an individual uses that will, to a great extent, determine whether his or her performance is one of mediocrity or excellence. Now let's dive even deeper below the surface here.

The productivity and ability to carry out a particular mental program is, to a large degree, determined by the physiological state of the individual or their frequency as we have been showcasing it throughout *The Reinvention Formula*. The level of arousal, receptivity, or perhaps the stress or anxiety of individuals will determine how effective they are at carrying out their own mental programs. Here's the kicker. It's an individual's internal state that has the influence on the ability to perform in any situation, especially brainstorming and strategizing. I feel this is one of the most eye-popping and important chapters for anyone who wants to accomplish something big and impactful. You must understand that you don't need to be born with a certain level of intelligence; you do, however, need to be resourceful, creative, and willing to elevate your internal state and frequency and be able to think outside of the box.

When I made the decision to begin CLS, I had that moment of imposter syndrome when that voice in my head said, "This is a saturated space. Everyone wants to be a coach or speaker. Why you? You won't stand out." I loved this voice, because it presented all the potential obstacles and challenges that would eventually come my way, and gave me an opportunity to jump on them before I even began reverse engineering this whole vision and getting ready to face any and all adversity that came my way. This was a strategy that gave me confidence, because I was essentially prepared for many of the challenges that it takes to power through to become the best in the world at what I was looking to do. Does that make me a genius? I'll let you decide that, but what it definitely did do was give me a visionary mindset, and I took pleasure in thinking outside the box just as I have seen so many of the pioneers and world shakers do, who I have mentioned in this chapter. You can use this same approach in any endeavor in life, not just a new career.

There is never a dead end in life. There are obstacles and challenges that we must figure out how to overcome. Sometimes there is a big wall in our path. We may have to crawl underneath, climb over it, or just plow right through it. But if you're willing to tap into your creative and divine energy, there is always a way. If not, then we build our own table and bring the world to us. For example, let's say you wanted to be a keynote speaker, but you weren't getting booked or presented with any opportunities. You can get resourceful and create your own event, build momentum, and eventually other events will either want to hire you or they will want to speak on your platform. That's just one example, but the point is there is always a way. Everything can be figured out, if you're willing and committed to your vision. Let's change the narrative from seeing saturation in a given space we want to enter, to looking at that as a massive opportunity, because we know that by saturation what that really means is that there is a market for it. It's only a matter of time before we figure out the *how*. J. K. Rowling once said "anything's possible if you've got enough nerve" and I couldn't agree more. If you believe with every ounce of you that you or your big idea needs to be heard, there is absolutely a way. Maybe we just haven't figured it out yet.

Ask Yourself: How can you disrupt or become a trailblazer in one area of your life?

Note

1. https://podcasts.apple.com/gb/podcast/everything-is-figureoutable-with-marie-forleo/id1533716044?i=1000600699555

34

Certainty

Certainty and self-belief will get you further than any degree or certification.
– Craig Siegel

CERTAINTY IS JUST plain knowing. When you believe in and trust yourself, there is no obstacle too big. No amount of genius, MBAs, PhDs from Harvard, not even being a good person will guarantee you true prosperity as much as certainty. Certainty is a superpower. This is not arrogance, it's an unwavering self-belief that comes from tapping into something bigger than yourself and possessing a tranquil yet radiating aura about yourself. It's that mindset that winners simply win. With an unwavering certainty, you are no longer at the mercy of every little thing that happens. You are not a firefighter constantly putting out fires and obstacles. You are in the driver's seat, and from that vantage point you look down on your problems instead of up at them. The fires become the rare exception rather than the rule. When you have certainty, it's as if the fires give up. Soon the fires become the background rather than the foreground. They are annoyances and not tragedies.

Certainty, confidence, and self-belief, all of which I possess, create a foundation for people that allows them to become hard to kill. Essentially as you cultivate this level of self-belief, you become unstoppable, because you know without any doubt that you will succeed regardless of setbacks and adversity. It's important to me to identify the difference between being confident and being cocky. There is a huge difference between the two. An unwavering self-belief and certainty come with a great deal of humility and kindness. You don't have to be both supremely confident and yet arrogant. I imagine a guy like Tom Brady, down six points with under two minutes to go and having possession of the ball, would feel confident and not cocky. That means he absolutely believes in his abilities and execution yet he's not going to act like the game is already won until they push the ball into the endzone.

When I reinvented myself and stepped into a whole new world in a new industry and a totally different landscape, I may have been inexperienced, but I remained certain of my maniacal drive to figure it all out, put in the reps, ask for help, and stay enthusiastic throughout the inevitable growing pains that come when you step into any new arena. I was not cocky or arrogant that I would be replacing Tony Robbins within two years; however, I was committed to becoming the best that I can, beat on my craft, lean into the season of grind, and—arguably most importantly—maintain a positive attitude throughout.

There are different tools we can practice to elevate our level of certainty and self-belief. You can use the NLP tool of modeling to absorb confident characteristics of people you admire. You can certainly take pride in your preparation, which absolutely breeds confidence. I like to repeat mantras that elevate my frequency and enhance my awareness. I read the book *48 Laws of Power* years back written by Robert Greene, and although I imagine that book is not for everyone, there were several key takeaways that I wrote down in my journal that helped me gain confidence. The book gives history lessons from real-life figures and certain strategies that were used to conquer obstacles and achieve success and how those tools were applicable today in certain situations such as business.

I want to reiterate that it's one of those works where you take what you like and leave the rest. There was a short passage that I wrote down that said this: "Throughout history, the greats have managed to work the strategy of the crown, believing so firmly in their own greatness that it became a self-fulfilling prophecy." Now, this statement really stuck out to me for several reasons. If you study the greats of history from back in the day, including conquerors and warriors, to recent trailblazers and visionaries such as Walt Disney and Steve Jobs, you begin to notice and appreciate certain qualities that separated them from the rest. An unwavering certainty that their idea or vision could change the world.

Look, if you believe your big idea can impact and contribute to the world, then it's your responsibility to bring it to fruition. I may have lacked experience in the online space and personal branding and public speaking in 2020, but I wasn't going to let that prevent me from thinking of all that could go right if I could just cultivate 20 seconds of courage and make CLS happen. Thank goodness my level of certainty and self-belief outweighed my imposter syndrome and lack of experience, because as of the writing of this book in December 2022, we have made a massive contribution and impact elevating and inspiring millions of people across all our platforms, and that is what it is all about for me and what it will always be about. Helping people see and fulfill their dreams and potential. The understanding that reinvention is available to anyone at any time, and it's my responsibility to help people get to a place where they step into their own power and change the world for the better. We all have gifts and we are all unique, special, and here for a reason. We need to raise our hands and cosign abundance.

You don't need proof of concept to walk with a swagger or cultivate confidence. In fact in my humble opinion, it's the opposite that creates greatness. First you change your thoughts, thus creating new beliefs about yourself. You become confident and certain of your abilities, and then, you attract the results. Confidence and certainty are contagious. People want to be around you, teammates want to play with you, prospects want to do business with you, and you become magnetic. Icon and trailblazer Suzanne Somers[1] and I had an instant classic of a conversation on the *CLS Experience* podcast. She referenced her time with the legendary Frank Sinatra when she did her residency in Las Vegas with him. She illustrated how Frank had this aura about him. Girls wanted to be with him and guys wanted to be around him. His tranquil and radiating vibe was attractive to both sexes. This is what I am talking about with an unwavering self-belief and certainty.

Trust me, these traits are learnable. It's a cool, calm, and collective aura in which you seem patient and not anxious because you're certain it will all work out for you eventually. You can practice this. It's not a talent that you either are or are not born with. Never display doubt, and always maintain that assured demeanor. Become overcome by self-belief. Maintain self-discipline. Practice being mindful in conversations. Perform eye contact, which displays confidence. Smile often. Cultivate a sense of humor, build rapport with people. You can practice in the elevator or at the coffee shop. I would suggest being well groomed. Remember that attraction isn't a choice. It's always good to form an emotional connection with people or—in my arena—with your audience. Always—and I do mean *always*—maintain a positive attitude that will send a signal to anyone and everyone that you are confident, reassured, and possess a good aura about you. That is what people tend to gravitate toward.

Your energy introduces you before you ever speak. You know those people who walk into a room and before they even utter a word, everyone seems to gravitate toward them with a level of curiosity and wonder. That's energy. This is something we all have the ability to cultivate. It begins with certainty of ourselves and an unwavering self-belief. This is an absolute game changer and I can't recommend working on this enough. Start with a smile and build from there.

Ask Yourself: How much from 1 to 10 do you believe in yourself? How can you raise this number?

Note

1. https://podcasts.apple.com/us/podcast/the-it-factor-with-suzanne-somers/id1533716044?i=1000532891362

35

Education

In the world of entrepreneurs, you don't need a college education. You need a proper education.

– Robert T. Kiyosaki

IN 2023 EDUCATION means different things to different people. For example, there are certain professions and careers that require a certain degree or college education. Becoming a doctor requires med school, exams, and most likely a residency before you can become a doctor or start your own practice. Becoming an airline and commercial pilot requires a bachelor's degree and the FAA-issued Airline Transport Pilot (ATP) certificate. Becoming a lawyer requires law school. The list goes on. However, to be an entrepreneur you don't need specific degrees or a college education. What you need is information, and, of course, the necessary personality traits to persevere during the inevitable setbacks and challenges. Those personality traits include grit, resilience, resourcefulness, and a maniacal drive. I want to be responsible here and illustrate based on where I am today what I needed. I did in fact graduate college, and for me college proved to be an invaluable experience mainly due to being on my own, learning independence, and cultivating street smarts and life experiences. Looking back now, did I need my college degree to be where I am at today? The answer is no.

I think we all should do what feels right to us as individuals, and there is no rule about whether college degrees or any degrees are necessary prerequisites for a good job as that may have been the case years ago. Nowadays, there is so much information available to you at your fingertips that there is literally no excuse for not succeeding or winning big. YouTube, Google, books, and podcasts are all free for you to explore and gain knowledge and wisdom from. You could find a career you are really interested in and ask to intern there. That way you can learn the ropes and get mentored by someone who is much further along on the journey than you. Mentorship and coaches are available for you as well as communities. You could read this book and learn how to be resourceful and build a personal brand with no degree required. You could pick up any of the old-school classics such as *Think and Grow Rich* by

Napoleon Hill and *Rich Dad Poor Dad* by Robert T. Kiyosaki and already have a head start in life. If you want to gain an education in any arena these days, you are literally one click away from doing a deep dive and hyper focusing on that subject. Within a month or two, you can gain a ton of wisdom.

I think it's important to let you know that, while going to college provides a priceless experience in certain areas, it is no longer a necessity to be successful, earn a lot of money, and make a massive impact on the world. I think it's important, too, for each person to do what's best for them but also to realize that if you wanted to do something with your life, the chances are high that you are one click or book away from cultivating an abundance of information on that career to give you the confidence and know-how to begin.

College is just one path to gaining an education. In 2023 it's certainly not the only option. Podcasts, books, and internships are other forms of education, and it really all depends on what career you are looking to break into. A lot of people pile up a ton of debt and don't necessarily learn information that is relevant to their passions in college, so I think it should be considered on a case-by-case basis. I will, however, say that the experience itself was beautiful and learning a sense of independence and street smarts also is extremely important in life. Choose wisely, but do what's best for you. The world is evolving and it's not the same landscape in 2023 as it was in the year 2000. So while I think college is great for many reasons, what I think is most important is cultivating an education that helps you grow toward pursuing your dreams and passions. If you train your mind, you gain the potential to learn all sorts of things such as financial literacy and specific career necessities, based on the direction you want to go.

Many of the industries that have become popular in which you can create a lot of wealth or make a massive impact, like real estate investing, all things entrepreneurial, and even Hollywood don't require degrees. They require information and tools to build skill sets to advance. The truth is that a majority of jobs do not really require a college degree, but they do require skills—both technical knowledge and so-called "soft skills" needed to relate to customers and co-workers.

Additionally, social media can help a great deal in creating a nontraditional type of resume. Without a degree, you need another way to convince hiring managers that you're interested in their field and have the skills necessary to do the job well. Your résumé is important, but please understand that you have limitless room to build your brand on social media. For instance, focus on the content you share, write, and post. Use it to prove your drive, passion, and industry knowledge.

Most importantly I think there is an old saying that I want to conclude this chapter with: It's not necessarily what you know, but rather who you know that could very well provide the opportunity of a lifetime for you to get you started on your journey and career. Relationship capital is priceless and one of the most important concepts I have developed, specifically since I started my entrepreneurial journey in 2020. Build rapport and be of service of others and people will help you. Be ready for that opportunity and always ask for help. If you're willing to work hard and be a sponge and possibly intern for the person that is sitting in the seat that you would eventually like to sit in, then your future is absolutely limitless and rich with potential. Be kind to others and always go the extra mile and doors will open. College is great but it's not a necessity depending on which path you'd like to take. The choice is yours.

Ask Yourself: Where do you need to allocate energy to become more educated in what you desire?

36

Dating Your Audience

Every battle is won before it is ever fought.

– *Sun Tzu*

"EVERY BATTLE IS won before it is ever fought." There is a very good reason that this quote is mentioned by many legends and business moguls across all arenas in life. It goes back to one of my favorite life mantras, preparation breeds confidence. I feel an inclination to pull back the curtain on how to win in sales and have a productive launch for any product or service you may be offering. So many online coaches try to work with me and they want all the secrets about how our CLS brand exploded, but the truth is I find way too many people wanting shortcuts and the "secret sauce." Let me be perfectly honest and transparent here. You have to date your audience first before you can launch your services and expect people to raise their hand and lock arms with you.

Here's an example I like to give. When I proposed to Olesya and took a knee, ring in hand, to ask her to be my wife and spend the rest of her life with me, did she say yes because on that particular day I had a nice button-down on and my hair looked freshly cut? (Side note, I refer to my haircut as my hairpiece. I told you I was weird.) No, of course she didn't make her decision based on how I showed up on that day alone. She said yes because of the prior 17 months of dating, building an intimate connection, and creating a foundation of a beautiful and amazing relationship.

So how is this any different from sales? You have to create that Hollywood hype, get to know your audience and see what they are in the market for. What can they use help with, what is something that they are missing that you can provide? How can you fill a void? The key to a successful business launch of any kind is to interact and engage with your target audience so that when you do in fact go to open up for business, you're not hoping and praying that people sign up. You already dated them and built a connection with them, finding out what they are in the market for.

Just as lead generation and sales conversion are arguably the bloodlines to any successful business, your mindset is 98% of the battle. Look at some of the biggest companies out there such as Apple, Amazon, and Disney. They collect data on how they can make the experience of working with them smoother and more effortless. For my fellow entrepreneurs and business owners out there, please take the time to get to know your audience and nurture those relationships. This is how you will consistently deliver and gain referral business, which is every business owner's dream. Just as you would date your partner and build that relationship before you proposed, it's the same mindset and concept for business. Collect the data and see what the people need help with and double down on that. With this strategy you'll never launch something and hear crickets, ya dig?

Ask Yourself: Where can you look for feedback in order to deliver a more optimal experience?

37

Imagine If

Think about everything that could possibly go right, and live in that bubble of serenity and watch what life delivers you.

— *Craig Siegel*

Two words that can make your wildest dreams come true, and two words that can haunt you for the rest of your life are "imagine if." Let's start with the latter.

Imagine if I gave in to imposter syndrome at the beginning of the pandemic and I never started CLS because I was inexperienced with the online space and didn't think people would be interested in my story. Well, then you wouldn't be on the road to reinvention by reading this book. Imagine if I didn't go on that date with Olesya because she was not my usual type that I typically dated in the past. Well, then I wouldn't have truly discovered what falling in love feels like on our way to planning a wedding and starting a family with my soul mate. Imagine if I didn't come back determined after my first two-mile run humbled and frustrated me. Well, then I wouldn't have begun to find myself again in this world and conquer six marathons, proving to myself that I can do hard things. You get the point here. Life is made up of imagine-if scenarios that could change the entire trajectory of your destiny.

Often, the biggest growth and life-altering magic occurs after you acknowledge the difficult choices and choose them anyway. I boldly suggest that you will never regret saying, "Hell, yes" to the uncomfortable but necessary growth choices in life. Done will always be better than perfect. I constantly get asked how I cultivated the courage to totally reinvent myself and pivot in the pandemic while appearing at the time to have a "stable job." The cost of inaction is the greatest cost of all. Here's where the magic of the two words *imagine if* comes into play.

Any time you're facing a difficult yet necessary choice or perhaps you're just doing your visualization exercise, ask yourself: "Imagine if?" Imagine if I start CLS, take the past 15 years of sharpening the ax and consuming my mental fitness and I package it to inspire the world? Imagine if it takes off and I start a podcast that would get sponsored by billionaire Mark Cuban, and I get to interview the world's most interesting and successful entrepreneurs, entertainers, movie stars, and professional athletes, and I become friends with them and coach many. Imagine if I develop the skills to become a charismatic, impactful, and top keynote speaker, speaking all around the world, including one particular venue with an audience of 70,000 within my second year in the industry. Imagine if I build a community inside the CLS Membership that attracts over 500 amazing humans inside an exclusive group within the second year and we're on our way to attracting thousands. Imagine if I make such an impact that I become available for amazing opportunities such as signing a massive book deal with the great Wiley publishing house and create this special and strategy-rich work that will change the world? Imagine if we show up daily, talking about how it's never too late to reinvent yourself and showcase the power of vulnerability and impact millions of people through all our platforms?

You see what we're getting at here? Imagine if your idea takes off and creates hybrids, and it makes a massive impact as well as making you a lucrative living, and you wake up every morning jazzed and excited about your career. Well, most people do in fact say to themselves, "Imagine if," it's just that they are so programmed to take the pessimistic and negative approach that they typically say, "Imagine if I fail," or "Imagine if people think I look stupid." The two-word combination of Imagine *if* changed my life, and it will change yours immediately, as long as you ask the question with a positive outlook. Imagine if it goes right?

You see, the very knowledge of our thoughts becoming things and that each thought has a frequency and its own energy behind it, should encourage you to begin asking positive questions to yourself. Imagine if I go to this event, and I meet someone who has a great opportunity for me or perhaps I meet a great guy or girl and that leads to a relationship? I see zero benefits from maintaining a negative mindset, because it thins your life to the glass being half empty. I do however see limitless opportunities and possibilities for those who dare to ask themselves what could go right? How good can you stand it?

As I'm writing this chapter, it's 4:30 a.m. in New York City. I am sitting on my obscenely oversized recliner in my living room with the stunning and gorgeous pink and orange skyline beginning to creep in behind me. I'm sipping on some delicious hot coffee, wearing my comfortable morning sweatshirt, and the movie *The Matrix* is on in the background. I always have something playing in the background that inspires me while I work. We just nailed a massive business goal that I had for the year and it's currently December 28, 2022. Hitting that massive goal tells me a few things. Number one, clearly I wasn't thinking or playing big enough, because, as I always like to teach, if your goals are being hit then they're probably too small. The truth is that when I set this goal this time last year, the goal scared me and made me feel anxious. That's the appropriate feeling for setting big audacious goals. However, what I did do this year, as I continue to evolve and become more advanced, is set the tone and the intention for the year, but then divorce from the outcome and simply not worry about the how. We smashed the goal and I am so proud of myself, the team, and CLS as a whole.

The most important thing here is that CLS continues to soar and as a result more lives are being elevated and changed for the better. We encourage all those who know deep down that they are here for more than they are currently doing to reinvent themselves and their lives at any moment. Sometimes we're looking for permission to totally change gears or think bigger and shoot for the stars. Here's the kicker. Imagine if I didn't put that massive goal in my 2022 journal entry and whiteboard because it made me feel uncomfortable and insecure.

The truth is, the power in setting massive goals in life is not actually the goal itself. It's who you become on the journey to be the type of cat that hits goals like that. I have become significantly better as a human this year in all areas of my life. I am more empathetic and compassionate. More experienced and skilled at my craft. More effective in coaching and leading thousands of people to elevate their own lives. A better boyfriend turned fiancé. A better son, brother, and uncle. A better businessman. A better listener. A better runner. A better servant leader. I have a significantly stronger relationship with God. I'm just better all around.

Part of the reason that I have made quantum leaps in all areas is because, by setting massive goals and intentions, I have forced myself to level up in all areas of life so that I can become the type of person who attracts this type of abundance into my life. You can too. What if you set those audacious goals and you become a more enhanced human being who actually nails those big goals? Start with that question and then lean into that journey, and watch all the magic unfold. Even if you come up short from your audacious goals, I imagine it's safe to say you will become a significantly better person in the process and find yourself much further ahead in a relatively short period of time, because, as they say, when you shoot for the moon, you may come up short and still land on the stars. Or is the saying the opposite? Either way you get the point. Dream Big. Play Big. Become better. Imagine if it all works out?

Ask Yourself: What is one thing that you can imagine working out for you that you previously thought was impossible?

38

This Is Your Movie

This is your movie. If you don't like the plot, change the script and replace the cast with more empowering characters.

– Craig Siegel

FOLLOW ME HERE. What if this life of yours is one big giant movie. Maybe you haven't loved the first or second act thus far. Everyone knows the best movies are the ones that stick the landing. That's why I was so upset when my favorite TV show, *Game of Thrones*, ended in a disappointing fashion by having a lackluster and forgettable final season. Sorry, *GOT* fans, I felt compelled to get that off my chest, but the truth is that show was incredible for seven seasons and ended sour. Your life presents the opportunity to do the opposite. What if the next year or 25 years could be your best yet? I mean I certainly lived more over the past 2 years than the previous 35 combined. Why can't you? Of course, you can. Let's start with acknowledging some of the issues with the film production, also known as your life, at the moment and how we can enhance the next act.

Who are the supporting characters in your movie? Do they elevate you or deplete you? Do they inspire you or take the wind out of your sails? Do they make you a better human being by being around them, or do they actually make you feel small and insignificant? If the people around you aren't making your movie better, it's time to do an audit and see which actors need to be fired and replaced with people who are in alignment with who you are becoming.

I've evolved and I am continuing to grow and shed old skins and identities. As a result, my movie continues to get an upgrade of supporting characters who best suit this season of life for me. Of course there are still people in my life from my past who I don't interact with as much anymore; I just make the conscious effort to be more selective with where I allocate my energy. I just want to be clear, this does not mean that I'm better or feel any type of way other than that as we continue to evolve it's only natural that you gravitate toward like-minded people who are on a similar path with similar goals.

You must come to terms with the fact that you cannot hang around people that are underachieving, and expect to win. Your vibe attracts your tribe. Additionally if you hang around winners long enough, you will learn how to win. Our time here is limited with regard to the human experience, so let's double down on being around the frequency of people who are growth oriented and doing great things. Consider keeping the conversations about the glory days limited.

Perhaps we're not 100% in love with the current plot in our movie. We work somewhere, but we know in our hearts and souls that we are here for more, or maybe the job is holding you back from something greater, more impactful, more soul feeding or even more lucrative. You have the power to change how the next scene plays out. Put yourself on LinkedIn or Indeed, give your profile a facelift, and get back out there to see what else is available. Perhaps you always wanted to start your own business and see where that leads to, cut out the Netflix and mindless television and begin dialing in on your side hustle. You see the ball is in your court. If you're alive, then the movie hasn't ended yet.

I looked at my movie at the end of 2019 heading into 2020 as my redemption arc. The hero's journey. Every great movie's main character goes through a fall and then the climb. Life is no different. Adversity, trauma, sometimes physical pain, and definitely emotional pain are part of every script, bar none. No one is exempt from the inevitable curveballs and heartbreaking setbacks. However, trust me when I tell you that pain may be inevitable but suffering is optional.

You see, awareness is one of the most powerful traits that we can cultivate. Admittedly I spent a bit too long feeling sorry for myself a few years back having found myself in a dark season, which should have been a moment and not a couple years. I wasn't available yet for my reinvention or plot twist and script rewrite. Hence, the core message of CLS is to bring that awareness, support, and strategies to help people become unstuck and start now. I have contrast. I also believe everything happened for a reason and exactly at the right moment for me, which is why CLS has been on this meteoric rise since inception. People think what we've created here has been an overnight success. I have been sharpening the ax for 15 years straight. I just finally was able to put it all together at the beginning of the pandemic. I had been setting the intention and then I had my spiritual awakening where I asked God to reveal himself in the most amazing ways, and then the blueprint for CLS began to flow through me.

The whole point of what we do here is to help people achieve their reinvention and success much quicker than I did. Just as one of my best friends and mentors, David Meltzer, always says, he already paid the dummy taxes and in some ways so did I. This book alone is a personal development guide, full of all the magic, nuggets, mindset, mental fitness, strategies, lessons and paradigm shifts that I have been working on for a decade and a half all organized and put into one vessel, called *The Reinvention Formula*.

Furthermore, let's say you are not in love with your body right now and you're 50 years young. You can decide right now that the script changes and you can put together the strategy to get in the best physical shape of your life and begin to love yourself again. Perhaps you're not in love with the cinematography of your movie; you do have the choice to change the geography and create a fresh start. Whether it's your career, where you live, your personality, your friends, or your current situation in general, the movie is not over yet, and you hold the pen to write your next scene. In fact, if need be, create an entirely new next act of the film. The choice is yours, and the movie analogy helped me a lot in realizing that a few years back, I wasn't actually stuck, I just thought I was. I stopped participating in the perception and I took accountability and ownership for my situation and forgave myself. Then, I got to work, the doors opened, and here we are. My movie looks like an entirely different film, genre, and cast from the way it appeared just two-and-a half years ago. I can't stress enough how much can change once you become available and lean in. Your movie—you decide how it ends.

Ask Yourself: What would be your preferred storyline of your next season of life?

39

Unlearn and Reinstall

Before we can reinvent ourselves, sometimes we have to unlearn all our past programming and install new empowering beliefs that present possibilities.

– Craig Siegel

MOST OF US are operating from a subconscious that has been developed since the time we were about five years old and we assume that this is how the world works. For example, my parents used to purposely not say something that we wanted to happen out loud, because they were superstitious and thought that if you said it, we would actually jinx the possibility of it happening. I love my parents more than anything, but now, having done so much work on myself and recreating myself like clay, I feel the opposite is much more effective. Setting our intentions and putting them out there for the universe is one of the greatest strategies that I had to first unlearn and then reinstall. This is how we manifest what we want. You crush big goals, by first setting the intention and then marrying the process. My amazing parents thought that the universe would make sure it didn't happen if we declared it. I respectfully disagree and feel the opposite is true now. It doesn't mean my parents were wrong and I am right, it's just what feels better for me and is significantly more effective for me creating a life of abundance. First, you have an idea that makes something a possibility. Then, you set the intent and take inspired action. And finally, it becomes a probability. That's one of the powers of intention.

Words are very powerful. Perhaps someone teased you when you were a kid and told you that you were ugly or that you were fat or that you had a bad voice even though you liked to sing. Now, you go through life adopting those beliefs and as a result never chase your dreams because those words hurt and discouraged you. However, what if you read this right now and realize that words are powerful but they are not facts. Then, you have the power to uninstall that belief and reinstall a more empowering one that gives you confidence and inspiration, and you now step into your power, utilize your gifts, and reinvent yourself and change your entire life the way I did.

Listen, it's time to win. If the scoreboard is currently showing that you're losing, then what do you want to do about it? It's not enough to just be a good human. You have an obligation to contribute and make a difference. It's our collective responsibility to shine bright, give others the permission to step up and show up authentically, and make an impact. We have to cultivate a sense of urgency to win and create a movie that best suits us and the world. That's my opinion at least. I once starred in a movie called *Existing*. Trust me, it was miserable. I wasn't happy or fulfilled, nor was I making any sort of contribution to the world but I acknowledged it and transformed. We all have that power. If you're reading this book, then your movie isn't over yet, and in my opinion, you're just getting warmed up. Forget about the current scoreboard or plot of the movie that doesn't feel up to par with what you know you are capable of. What are you going to do now to change the next scene and make the next moment the best moment of your life? You're not just the main character in your movie, you're also the director. Create as you see fit and let's have some fun.

Unlearning many habits and programs that we have been using for most of our lives doesn't have to be as challenging as you may think. Think of a computer program that has a glitch or is causing your device to perform slowly. You may delete it and reinstall a new one that has no bugs or glitches, and your device will immediately begin to perform faster and smoother. Begin to think of your life like that as well. Thoughts and words are not facts. Imposter syndrome or someone's negative criticisms of you are not proven facts; they are just there. Take responsibility for being able to unemotionally delete and remove those stories, and replace them with a whole new positive thought and belief. If you are not currently where you want to be in life, it's most likely because of a story that is replaying in your head that you began to believe. Typically, it's a fear of failure or what other people may think. You were not born with that programming, so as long as you can acknowledge that, then you can step inside any arena with confidence and a mindset full of opportunities and possibilities. If you believe you can't approach the handsome guy at the bar because you lack confidence or you think he may reject you or you feel society says the girl can't approach the guy, then you can choose to believe that and continue on with your life with those painful "Imagine if's" or you can choose a different thought and showcase confidence and say society doesn't dictate how you operate and go over there and see what happens. That's just one analogy. I could give a million.

My friends, we can make the choice to let go of any and all limiting beliefs and previous stories that have been holding us back, keeping us stuck in our comfort zone, or, worse, suffering in silence. We can buy into the perceptions that we may look silly trying something that we lack experience in, or we can participate in the perception that everyone was once a beginner and you have to start somewhere in order to ascend to new heights and your amazing dream life. Which perception do you want to partake in? Let me give you an example here. I participated in victim mentality and unworthiness for a few years. You know where that got me? Absolutely nowhere except deeper into my rabbit hole of feeling sorry for myself combined with a whole lot of underachieving. Then, I had an awakening. I realized that I was here for much more than I was currently settling for, so I became available and pursued something that I loved backed by determination and creativity. One story was slow, miserable, and unproductive. The other story was blissful, impactful, exhilarating, and abundant. It was still Craig. I just changed which programs I was subscribing to and I reinstalled the ones that actually helped and empowered me. It's not easy but it's simple.

The choice is yours, but please understand that many of the programs that have been running in our brain have been conditioned and compounded over time to the point that we don't even realize we're running the program. Awareness is the key here. Acknowledgment means that we are presented with the choice. Let the unproductive programs continue, or uninstall and reinstall. Let's be intentional with our mental computer and double down on the programs and stories that help us change the world.

Ask Yourself: What current conditioning do you need to uninstall?

40

Ego

You can either be a host to God, or a hostage to your Ego. It's your call.
— *Wayne Dyer*

THE INFAMOUS EGO and all the different perspectives about it. New York Mets legend Darryl Strawberry[1] said to me on *The CLS Experience* that ego stands for Easing God Out. I thought that was beautiful coming from a man who made one of the most impressive reinventions that I have ever seen firsthand. When you're operating from your ego you tend to be in fight or flight mode. You find yourself analyzing everything and you certainly aren't aware or actually present. That's not who you really are, because from this frequency you are not expansive, you are limited, essentially buying into scarcity. You're worried and anxious and definitely not abundant and effortless. A great way to eliminate this low vibration is to be super mindful and present in any given moment. Bring all the energy back to who and where you are—straight love, energy, and connection. Our ego often makes us create the need to be offended, or that we have to be right. Our ego prevents us from asking for help because we think we can do it alone. Our ego says look at me, as opposed to come with me. Our ego wants us to take center stage or assume a sense of vanity. Our ego is essentially our opponent, always trying to prevent us from being one with the universe or infinitely full of possibilities.

Here's a paradigm shift. What if it was actually the opposite? What if our ego was our friend because any time we heard its unproductive voice in our heads, we immediately knew that we needed to become aware and take a step back? What if our ego was the 3D world, also known as reality, and disconnecting from our ego meant the realm of infinite possibility also known as the quantum or the vortex? Remember, thoughts are not facts and the ego is a trickster. Any time we have a limiting belief, that's the ego trying to keep us from shining bright and existing loudly. People often think to themselves "Who am I to start something brand new?" I challenge you to think, "Who are you not to try something new and exciting?"

The ego could be interpreted as temptation, similar to the snake in the Garden of Eden where Adam and Eve were seduced to take a bite of the forbidden fruit. Let's make an effort to become more mindful. We have to stop participating in a world where we are not enough and instead choose the world where we are more than enough. Dr. Daniel Amen beautifully articulated this on our episode of *The CLS Experience* where he suggested to challenge your limiting beliefs. This really stuck with me.[2] Your ego creates disempowering thoughts. These thoughts may include something along the lines of "I'm terrible with money" or "I'm lazy" or even "I'm unattractive," which causes self-destructive behaviors. This is dangerous because the ego can trap you and this tends to lead to some people succumbing to this permanently. We have the choice. In order to heal it, you have to feel it. Then we can choose to shed the ego. Thanks for coming! Let go of the ego and let God in—or the universe or whatever your belief is. Replace the ego with that. Double down on that. Practice awareness and resistance to giving in to your ego.

The big breakthrough for me was a concept I learned in Kabbalah, which is an esoteric method, discipline and school of thought in Jewish mysticism. This big powerful lesson taught me that anytime I feel a sense of temptation also known as the ego, it's an opportunity to resist that temptation and gain more spiritual light than if the temptation wasn't there to begin with. Bottom line, when you feel the ego, recognize it as an opportunity to resist, and this very game of temptation and resistance creates more divine spiritual energy in our lives. Enjoy that game changer and thank me later!

Ask Yourself: How can you get better at dealing with your ego?

Notes

1. https://podcasts.apple.com/us/podcast/turn-the-season-around-with-darryl-strawberry/id1533716044?i=1000571154591
2. https://podcasts.apple.com/gb/podcast/change-your-brain-every-day-with-dr-daniel-amen/id1533716044?i=1000604019563

41

The End Is Just the Beginning

*Now this is not the end. It is not even the beginning of the end. But it is,
perhaps, the end of the beginning. I believe this is where we are today.*

— Winston Churchill

LET'S LAND THE plane with the simple concept that all the stories, lessons, principles, methodologies, and strategies illustrated in this book are just the ammunition that you need to go into battle and succeed. You can, but will you? Will you apply everything we have learned and showcased inside *The Reinvention Formula*? Well, that's up to you. When making it real for yourself, consider the cost of inaction or, as I like to call it, the COI. How big a price do you pay choosing to live in mediocrity or, worse, unfulfillment, and unhappiness? I played that game for a few years, and although I know it was part of my journey, trust me when I tell you that I went through it so that you don't have to. It's reinvention season baby, and when you decide that you're here for more than you are currently doing, you become available for all of it. The career that lights up your soul, the perfect significant other, the moments of bliss, the quantum leaps, the timely miracles, and all the impact, contribution, and money you could ever dream of. I know it's hard to take action at times, but once you take one positive step, the seas begin to part and momentum begins. You got this. Don't give up and never surrender. You are valuable, you are blessed, and your gifts are important for the world. The only way you actually lose, is if you don't try. Look around you. Are there people that are winning big? Of course there are. Are they better than you? Not a chance! They're just further ahead. If they can do it, so can you.

At some point this human experience will come to an end. Our legacy and impact, however, will last forever. Failure is not an option, and with the proven tools discussed in *The Reinvention Formula*, you already possess the blueprint to upgrade your identity, reinvent yourself, and cultivate a bulletproof mindset. If you ever feel less than worthy or not ready to make moves, remember this. Ready is not a feeling; it's a decision. If all else fails, look yourself in the mirror and say these three words: Why Not You?

Ask Yourself: Why Not You?

Acknowledgments

I WANT TO acknowledge the CLS community, who have hopped on this rocketship and allowed me to pour into them with love, inspiration, strategies, and support and who have equally showed up for me and given me energy to fly higher each and every day. Our community is one of a kind, and the support and love that is both given and received is unmatched. We're all about growth, helping each other, and, of course, reinvention. We're here to put a dent in the universe and make a massive impact while unapologetically making a lot of money so that we can do great things with it. Without the rapidly growing love and support of the community, CLS would have never taken off the way it has. I acknowledge you, I see you, I feel you, and I love you all. The best is yet to come. Buckle up.

About the Author

Craig Siegel is a value-based and high-energy Global Keynote Speaker and rising thought leader, as featured in *Entrepreneur* and endorsed by some of the world's most well-known celebrities, entertainers, athletes, and entrepreneurs, such as Rob Dyrdek, Ed Mylett, Frank Grillo, Andy Grammer, Marie Forleo, Dr. Shefali, Tom Bilyeu, Bethany Hamilton, Suzanne Somers, Alicia Silverstone, Eric Thomas, Darryl Strawberry, NFL Hall of Famers Brian Dawkins and Edgerrin James, and more.

Craig is a born-and-raised New Yorker, who from a young age always knew that he was meant for more but was unable to put it all together. When the pandemic happened, Craig felt spiritually guided. He left his lucrative and comfortable job on Wall Street and went all-in with his passion and purpose to help people upgrade their mindsets and fulfill their potential. Craig's unique combination of energy, motivation, inspiration, charisma, and business success has led to the meteoric rise of **Cultivate Lasting Symphony (CLS)**, a contagious, never-before-seen explosion that has impacted millions of lives worldwide.

Removing limiting beliefs is the key to success in all areas of life. Most people feel unworthy. Craig helps people release the negative beliefs they have cultivated over time and implement positive and constructive thoughts, which then create powerful and positive beliefs that change your behaviors and ultimately create brand-new results in your relationships, business, and all facets of life. He illustrates the power of the second thought.

Index